Rent Control

Rent Control

A Case For

Herbert L. Selesnick
Harbridge House, Inc.

Lexington Books
D.C. Heath and Company
Lexington, Massachusetts
Toronto   London

Library of Congress Cataloging in Publication Data

Main entry under title:
  Rent control.

  "Study . . . conducted by the professional staff of Harbridge House, Inc. for the Massachusetts Joint Legislative Committee on Local Affairs, pursuant to House Nos. 5937 and 7866 of 1973 and 5798 of 1974."
  Bibliography: p.
  1. Rent control–Massachusetts. 2. Housing–Massachusetts. I. Selesnick, Herbert L. II. Harbridge House, Inc. III. Massachusetts. General Court. Joint Legislative Committee on Local Affairs.
HD7303.M4R45   333.5'4   75-31290
ISBN 0-669-00338-7

Copyright © 1976 by D.C. Heath and Company.

All rights reserved. No part of this publication may be reproduced or transmitted in any form or by any means, electronic or mechanical, including photocopy, recording, or any information storage or retrieval system, without permission in writing from the publisher.

Published simultaneously in Canada.

Printed in the United States of America.

International Standard Book Number: 0-669-00338-7

Library of Congress Catalog Card Number: 75-31290

For Judy, Marcy, and Julie

Contents

	List of Figures	ix
	List of Tables	xi
	Acknowledgments	xiii
	Introduction	xv
Chapter 1	**Statistical Evidence**	1
	Major Issues	1
	Detailed Analysis	2
Chapter 2	**Local Administration of Chapter 842**	41
	Introduction	41
	Conclusions	41
	Experience with Chapter 842–Brookline	44
	Experience with Chapter 842–Somerville	58
	Experience with Chapter 842–Cambridge	63
	Experience with Chapter 842–Boston	72
Chapter 3	**Fair Net Return**	87
	Purpose	87
	Statutory Framework	87
	Basic Similarities in Computing Rent Levels	88
	Computation of FNOI	89
	Comparative Analysis of the Various Methods	98
Appendix A	**Chapter 842 of the Acts of 1970**	103

Notes	115
Bibliography	117
About the Author	119

List of Figures

1-1	Percent Increase in Median Income and Median Rent Between 1960 and 1970 (Based on U.S. Census Figures) by City or Town	18
1-2	Prime Interest Rate, U.S. Residential Construction, and New England Residential Construction, 1968 to 1974	32

List of Tables

1-1	Estimated Rent Increases, 1970 to 1974	3
1-2	Apartment Vacancy Rate from Postal Vacancy Surveys (Percent of Total Apartments Unoccupied)	6
1-3	Rental Housing Association and Postal Vacancy Survey Data	7
1-4	Vacant Units in Boston's Public Housing	8
1-5	1970 U.S. Census Vacancy Rate for Rental Units by Rent Range	10
1-6	Massachusetts Housing Finance Agency Rental Statistics as of September 1974	12
1-7	Weekly Earnings of Factory Production Workers in Boston	14
1-8	Consumer Price Index for Urban Wage Earners and Clerical Workers in the Boston Metropolitan Area (1967 = 100)	15
1-9	Median Gross Rent per Month	16
1-10	Median Family Income, 1959 and 1969	17
1-11	Maintenance, Property Taxes, Total Expenses, and Net Operating Income as a Percentage of Valuation	20
1-12	Real Estate and Personal Property by Valuation which Is Tax Exempt	24
1-14	Valuation of Tax-Exempt Real Estate Property, 1973	25
1-15	Estimated Full Value Tax Rate (if Assessment Ratio = 100%)	26

1-16	Assessor's Data	27
1-17	Eckert's Analysis of Form 150 Data (Official Abatement Record of the Town of Brookline)	28
1-19(a)	Construction Activity: Value of Construction Contracts for Residential Buildings (Not Seasonally Adjusted)	33
1-19(b)	Financial Indicators (Seasonally Adjusted)— Savings on Deposit	33
1-19(c)	Real Estate Loans (Seasonally Adjusted)	33
1-20	Permits Issued for Multi-family Units: 1968-73	35
1-21	Number of Dwelling Units by Completion Year and by Financing in Boston	36
1-22	Dwelling Units Authorized by Building Permits, Structures with Three or More Units	37
1-23	Summary Process (Eviction) Writs Entered in Selected District Courts	38
1-24	Administrative Functions—Time Span	40
2-1	Summary of Civil Litigation in Brookline	55
2-2	Summary of Criminal Prosecution Activity in Brookline	58
2-3	Building Permit Statistics in Somerville	60
2-4	Proposed Budget and Staffing for DCA Bureau of Rental Housing	66
2-5	Range of Fair Returns	79
3-1	Allowable "Pass Through" Costs	90
3-2	Methods for Determining Fair Net Operating Income	91
3-3	Unit Cost of Local Rent Control Administration	112

Acknowledgments

This study was conducted by the professional staff of Harbridge House, Inc. for the Massachusetts Joint Legislative Committee on Local Affairs, pursuant to House Nos. 5937 and 7866 of 1973 and 5798 of 1974, which authorized the committee to conduct an investigation of the control of rents and evictions in the cities and towns of Massachusetts. Those staff members who made significant research, written, and review contributions were Adele G. Fleet, Susan G. Signore, Rosalind Y. Hammond, and Henry H. Norwood.

A multitude of government agencies and private organizations gave us access to documents and data. However, we wish to make particular note of the outstanding assistance we received from the following administrators of local rent control programs: William Edgerton and James Oliver, Boston; Roger Lipson, Brookline; J. Kenneth Griffin, Cambridge; and Lee Madigan and Andrew Brahm, Somerville. These individuals shared extraordinary amounts of their time and experience with us, and we are grateful to them.

Emily Achtenberg of Urban Planning Aid, Inc. contributed valuable statistical insights to this study and provided an important critical review of our effort.

We are also indebted to the Joint Chairmen of the Committee on Local Affairs, Senators Arthur Lewis and Stephen McGrail and Representative Donald Gaudette, as well as to the other committee members for their guidance in identifying important avenues of inquiry and for introducing a policy realism to our findings.

Consuelo Villegas provided able and tireless secretarial and editorial support in both the preparation of this book and the original study for the Joint Committee on Local Affairs. Special thanks are due to her for her outstanding administrative assistance.

Harbridge House has been privileged to participate in a study of such broad economic and social significance. It is our earnest hope that this report will contribute to a better understanding of rent regulation in the commonwealth.

Herbert L. Selesnick

Introduction

Purpose of the Study

This study was designed and conducted for legislative decision makers. In the Fall of 1974, the Massachusetts Joint Legislative Committee on Local Affairs was faced with the task of recommending to the full legislature either to allow the state's four-year old local option enabling statute for rent and eviction controls (Chapter 842 of the Acts of 1970) to expire, or to extend the statute and, if so, determine its form. Harbridge House was asked by the committee to assemble and analyze all the available data on the statute's impact since its inception and to formulate specific recommendations for the committee's consideration. Because the committee's mandate for this investigation was due to expire at the end of calendar year 1974, the study and report had to be completed within a four-month period.

Methodology

Opponents of Chapter 842 had been making the following allegations:

1. There is no longer the "emergency" shortage of decent affordable housing for the inhabitants of the commonwealth which formed the original rationale for passage of Chapter 842.

2. Rent control under Chapter 842 has had disastrous economic effects on local Massachusetts communities, including erosion of the tax base, cessation of new construction, housing deterioration, and condominium conversion.

3. The provisions of Chapter 842, as well as the local administration of rent control, have failed to allow adequate rent increases and profit levels for owners. Rents in controlled units have not kept pace with operating costs, and local rent board formulas have failed to provide mechanisms for adequate compensation. Complex rent board procedures and overemphasis on individual hearings have left thousands of units without rent increases and have been devastatingly unfair to small property owners.

To make maximum use of the limited time and resources available for the legislature's study, we decided that our research and analysis should focus on the confirmation or disconfirmation of these allegations. First and foremost, the study would have to be designed to answer the question of whether, in fact, there exists a *continuing* shortage of decent, affordable housing for inhabitants of the commonwealth and, if so, whether the magnitude and severity of this shortage are substantial enough to warrant the continued statutory provision of a local option for comprehensive regulation of rents and evictions.

It seemed to us that the only defensible way to answer this fundamental question would be with hard facts and figures showing (1) the magnitude, extent, and geographic distribution of the rental housing shortage in the commonwealth, if any, and (2) the types of people (poor, elderly, minorities, working class, etc.) who are suffering most from the shortage. One obvious symptom of a housing shortage is rapidly rising rents, which in many cases may also mean that tenants are having to spend an inordinate percentage of their income for rent and (in some cases) an inadequate amount for other necessities, such as food and clothing. The percentage of rental housing in a community that is vacant, but ready for occupancy, gives an added idea of how tight the housing market is. A low vacancy rate—perhaps less than five percent—indicates that a serious shortage exists. Substandard conditions may constitute additional evidence of a tight housing market and a housing shortage.

With these factors in mind, we structured our analysis of the availability of rental housing around the following key indicators:

1. Rent increases.
2. Rent-income ratios.
3. Vacancy rates.
4. Substandard housing.

Important sources of data on these key housing shortage indicators included the U.S. Government Printing Office, the Massachusetts Department of Community Affairs, the U.S. Post Office Survey, the Boston Area HUD Office, the Metropolitan Area Planning Council, local planning agencies, and local housing and redevelopment authorities.

Using these and other data sources, we have tabulated rent increases, rent-income ratios, vacancy rates, and substandardness for the rent-controlled communities within the state and for the state as a whole. Wherever possible, we have also produced breakouts by rent range. In addition, wherever possible, we have displayed these tabulations as a time series. For example, for 1968, 1969, 1970, 1971, 1972, and 1973, we show the impact of rent control and factor out special conditions in individual years that may have influenced housing availability more than the presence or absence of rent control. We have also prepared some of these tabulations for uncontrolled communities (1) to compare controlled and uncontrolled communities over the same period of time, and (2) to identify the possible degree of need for some form of rent control in noncontrolled communities. For the latter purpose, we have included some localities with less than 50,000 population in the sample of noncontrolled communities.

Once having determined the relative availability of low- and moderate-income level rental units, it was clear that we would have to address the question of what effect the rent and eviction control law has had on the cities and towns of the commonwealth that have adopted it. This requirement involved an assessment of Chapter 842's impact on the size and maintenance of the rental housing stock in each community that has adopted rent control, primarily by means of a comparison with those aspects of the rental housing stocks in other parts of the state. Wherever possible, we have broken the analysis down further into rent ranges and government-subsidized construction versus privately financed construction. A second major part of the impact evaluation involved an identification of the effect, if any, on the property tax structure in cities and towns due to their adoption of rent control. A major concern here was with finding out whether abatements for controlled cities and towns for controlled rental properties have been increasing faster than abatements in noncontrolled areas. (This phenomenon could indicate an assessing procedure aimed at rental income rather than property value and would suggest a possible "hidden cost" of rent control.)

The third major area of inquiry in this study was the administrative practices and procedures of local rent control boards and administrations. The intent of this part of our investigation was to focus on current problems with the administration of Chapter 842 at the local level and to suggest some possible solutions. To accomplish this objective, we gathered detailed information on items such as current case backlogs of local rent control boards/administrations, average time taken to process cases (by type of case—such as rent adjustment, eviction, etc.), procedures for maintaining order in hearings, and the degree of bias either toward landlords or tenants on the part of the board/administration.

Our methodology for describing local rent control administrative procedures and problems consisted primarily of on-site research in the form of in-depth interviews and document review. Persons interviewed in each of the controlled communities included members of rent control boards, local landlord and tenant representatives, and local elected and administrative officials. In addition, we talked with representatives of statewide landlord and tenant associations to obtain a comparative perspective on local administrative problems. The kinds of documentation we reviewed included applications from landlords and tenants for some form of relief, writeups of administrative actions taken by rent control boards, minutes of hearings and local press coverage since the adoption of rent control, as well as local rent control ordinances and associated administrative regulations.

On the basis of this type of on-site research in each of the controlled communities, we have prepared a profile of each community's rent and eviction control practices and procedures, highlighting major administrative issues and operating problems.

The second major focus of our local administrative analysis involved an exploration of the feasibility of defining and administering a fair net return formula for controlled properties. Chapter 842 guarantees landlords a so-called "fair net operating income," which is supposed to give them a "fair profit" or "fair return" on their investment. It is up to rent-control officials to decide just which this means, however. The law specifies the following factors as some to be considered in determining whether a controlled rental unit yields a fair net operating income:

1. Increase or decrease in property taxes.
2. Unavoidable increase or decrease in operating and maintenance expenses.
3. Capital improvement of the housing unit, as distinguished from ordinary repair, replacement, and maintenance.
4. Increase or decrease in living space, services, furniture, furnishings, or equipment.
5. Substantial deterioration of the housing units other than as a result of ordinary wear and tear.
6. Failure to perform normal repair, replacement, and maintenance.

Although the enabling law has basic standards and procedures which the city or town must follow, there is wide latitude for local interpretation. For example, it is up to local rent-control officials to decide what kinds of operating expense increases justify a rent increase. The ultimate impact of rent control at the local level therefore depends on the kind of regulations the local rent control board adopts and how it enforces those regulations. The decision about fair net operating income is perhaps the most important one the rent control board makes. It determines a lot about how high rents will be and the relative benefits received by landlords and tenants under the rent-control system.

In assessing the feasibility of developing and administering a fair net return formula, we have considered the relative merits of the following major types of formulas:

1. Value formula (fair net operating income is the percentage rate of return on value of the property).
2. Gross rent formula (fair net operating income is the percentage of total rents charged in the building).
3. Equity formula (the fair net operating income is the percentage rate of return on the landlord's actual cash investment in the property).
4. Dollar net operating income formula (fair net operating income is the net operating income in some base year plus some percentage factor for inflation).

In evaluating the advantages and disadvantages of these and other formulas, we have used the following general criteria:

1. Is the formula easy to understand and administer?
2. Does the formula discourage rapid resale and speculation and encourage long-term stable ownership?

3. Does the formula reduce or stabilize inflated property values?
4. Does the formula encourage good maintenance and improvements?

There are many variations in each of the major types of formulas and ways that they can be combined. Each type of formula has its own particular problems, and we have explored these in the course of the study. On the basis of this comparative analysis, we have rendered a judgment as to the administrative feasibility of a fair net return formula.

To sum up, our study methodology consisted of the following major steps:

1. Collection and analysis of available statistical evidence related to the major arguments and allegations for and against Chapter 842.
2. Determination of whether the available evidence supports conclusively one or the other set of assertions.
3. Evaluation of the local administrative experience with Chapter 842 and assessment of the feasibility of defining a fair net return formula.
4. Formulation of conclusions and recommendations about the extension or expiration of Chapter 842, based on the available evidence as to its impact and its administrative feasibility.

Principal Conclusions

The following is a summary of our major findings:

Rent Increases

1. Since the inception of rent control, average residential rent has increased by 27.6 percent in the greater Boston area. In the four communities now operating under Chapter 842, average rent has risen only 16.0 percent since 1970.

2. A study of Boston rent-control decisions concludes that one out of three rent-increase petitions was granted in full. One out of three received partial increases "substantially short" of what had been requested. One-fifth of all rent-increase petitions were flatly denied.

Vacancy Rates

1. No reliable measure of vacancy rates in Massachusetts communities currently exists. An accurate indicator of vacancy rates must give a breakdown of vacant units by size, rent range, condition, and location.

2. Existing market studies yield a wide range of conclusions about current vacancy rates, but all studies support the conclusion that there is a shortage of low- and moderate-cost rental housing in many urban communities of the commonwealth and in some small communities as well.

3. Public housing in Massachusetts urban cities and towns have very few vacant units, except for Boston where 61 percent of all vacant public units are in Roxbury and Dorchester.

4. Waiting lists for low-income and elderly public units are several years long.

5. Census data on vacancy rates include unoccupied but substandard units. The exclusion of dilapidated and deteriorated rental housing from these surveys would significantly decrease their estimates of vacancy rates. This effect is especially significant in Boston and Cambridge.

Cost of Living

1. Real income of tenants in the Boston metropolitan area declined during 1974.

2. The cost of buying a home in the greater Boston area has risen faster than the cost of residential rent annually since 1968. Therefore low- and moderate-income families find it increasingly difficult to leave the rental housing market as the gap widens between renting and owning.

3. During the ten-year period preceding rent control, Massachusetts median family income rose 73 percent. In rent-controlled communities, however, median family income rose only 63 percent from 1960 to 1970.

4. During the ten-year period preceding rent control, median rent rose an average of 57 percent in communities which subsequently adopted Chapter 842. The median rent in Massachusetts, however, rose only 20 percent.

5. Between 1967 and 1970, the average cost of fuel oil and coal rose 8.5 percent in the greater Boston area. Between 1970 and 1974,[a] the average cost rose 88.7 percent in the greater Boston area.

6. Between 1967 and 1970, the average cost of gas and electricity rose 5.6 percent in the greater Boston area. Between 1970 and 1974,[a] the average cost rose 40.3 percent in the greater Boston area.

Property Taxes

1. With the exception of Boston, tax rates rose more slowly in rent-controlled communities since the adoption of Chapter 842 than in 17 noncontrolled urban cities and towns in the commonwealth.

---

[a]The average cost for 1974 was calculated as the mean of the January, April, July, and October consumer price indices.

In Boston, where 59 percent of all real estate is currently tax-exempt, the tax rate rose 61 percent during 1970-1973.[b]

2. In rent-controlled communities, if property taxes exceed 30 percent of a landlord's gross revenue, he or she will petition for and receive an abatement from the local assessor or the Appellate Tax Board. Because the tax board consistently grants such petitions, local assessors in rent-controlled communities now settle at 30 percent, avoiding costly litigation at the appellate level.

3. Brookline data shows that the impact on that town's tax rate of abatements to rent-controlled properties represented only $0.53 in 1970, $0.48 in 1971, and $0.29 in 1972.

4. Rent-controlled properties which received both a rent adjustment and an abatement of property tax had a much smaller impact on Brookline's tax rate than properties without rent adjustments which received abatements.

5. The above finding is true, in general, for any rent-controlled community which allows landlords to "pass through" property taxes to tenants.

New Construction

1. Some Boston area bankers refuse to underwrite mortgages in rent-controlled cities and towns. Other bankers would underwrite such mortgages if mortgage money were currently available. Loan money at reasonable interest rates is difficult to obtain in any urban community, independent of the presence or absence of rent control.

2. 54 percent more multifamily units were built between 1971 and 1973 than between 1968 and 1970 in rent-controlled communities. For the 17 noncontrolled communities, 39 percent more multifamily units were built between 1971 and 1973 than between 1968 and 1970.

3. Construction as reflected by permits issued of subsidized housing in noncontrolled communities increased by 47 percent between 1971 and 1973 in relation to its 1968 through 1970 rate. Construction of subsidized housing as reflected by permits issued in rent-controlled communities increased by 69 percent between 1971 and 1973 in relation to its 1968 through 1970 rate.

4. The nationwide rate of new subsidized housing construction has dropped significantly since 1971, with structures having *five* or more units experiencing the sharpest decline.

5. The nationwide rate of new privately owned housing construction has also declined significantly since 1972.

Maintenance of Rental Property

1. Statistical data are inconclusive regarding the level of housing code enforcement in rent-controlled communities.

---

[b]Boston's acceptance of Chapter 842 became effective on January 1, 1973. There have been no major increases in Boston's tax rate since that time.

2. Maintenance as a percentage of rent increased in Brookline during the first three years of rent control.

Rent Control Administrative Costs, Time Lag for Decisions, and Evictions

1. The annual administrative costs of rent control per controlled unit ranged from a minimum of $4.32 in Somerville to a maximum of $12.81 in Brookline during 1974.

2. The average length of time between filing a petition and receiving a decision from the rent control board ranges from 4 to 5 weeks in Somerville to 10 to 12 weeks in Brookline.

3. *Eviction.* Eviction writs entered in district courts decreased substantially in rent-controlled communities, proving that Chapter 842 protects tenants from being evicted without just cause.

The statistical evidence and local administrative experiences analyzed in this study indicate that there is no sound justification for allowing the expiration of Chapter 842. None of the available data demonstrate that Chapter 842 has significantly impaired the supply or quality of rental housing or contributed materially to the erosion of local tax bases. Despite some serious startup problems which affected all of the rent-controlled communities, the calibre of local rent-control administration has been improving steadily with each year's experience under Chapter 842. We found absolutely no evidence either of widescale administrative abuses of the statute by local boards and administrators or of excessively large backlogs of unprocessed cases. On the contrary, each of the rent-controlled communities has developed an impressive degree of systematization for the processing of adjustments and evictions. Some fair net return formulas have clear advantages over others in terms of equity between landlord and tenant, effectiveness in controlling rents, and administrative ease of application. The differences, however, which produce these advantages are often ones of degree and would appear better dealt with through administrative regulations rather than statutory changes. State level guidelines are needed—which address in some detail both the computation of fair net return and the determination of the types and amounts of allowable cost pass-throughs—to assure at least a minimum level of consistency, to avoid a "reinventing of the wheel" and repetition of the same mistakes by each municipality, and to provide a structure for building a body of consistent and supportive court decisions. Also in this regard, there is an important function that the Massachusetts Department of Community Affairs might logically perform in developing an appropriate statistical data base of rent trends and landlord cost increases in the commonwealth.

Organization of Results

The following pages describe our research techniques in greater detail, setting forth the resultant findings, conclusions, and recommendations in separate and independent sections on the available statistical evidence, local administrative practices, and fair net return formulas.

Rent Control

1 Statistical Evidence

The statistical evidence presented in this chapter was assembled in order to shed light on some of the issues raised in landlord and tenant interviews. For many issues, our analysis of the impact of rent control was hampered by the unavailability of recent data. In several analyses we have relied upon our own sampling of current data to draw conclusions. We collected extensive statistical evidence from rent control board files; federal, state and municipal agencies; planning councils; private research organizations; landlords and tenants; and others. Occasionally sources were reluctant to provide available data to us. In several cases pertinent statistical data were not scheduled to be compiled by the appropriate agencies until after the completion of this study.

The major arguments for and against rent control raised by landlords, tenants, and others translate into the following issues.

Major Issues

1. *The degree of success with which rent control has stabilized rent levels.* Prior to the adoption of Chapter 842, were rents rising faster than income? Since the adoption of rent control have rents risen more slowly in rent-controlled communities than in noncontrolled communities? How often do landlords receive the full amount requested in a petition for a rent increase? What are the average rent levels in controlled communities? What are the average rents paid by tenants in public housing?

2. *The current vacancy rates of rental housing in both rent-controlled and noncontrolled communities.* Is there currently a shortage of rental housing, or is there an adequate supply of vacant rental units? How long are waiting lists for public housing? How is the vacancy rate affected statistically by the inclusion of substandard unoccupied units?

3. *The effect of inflation on the cost of living.* How do recent changes in tenants' incomes compare with recent changes in rents? Have rents risen faster than the cost of buying a home? How quickly is the cost of fuel and utilities rising?

4. *The impact of rent control upon local tax rates.* Does rent control cause the tax rate to increase? What percentage of a landlord's gross revenue is represented by property taxes? Does rent control cause an increase in abatements to rental properties? Do such abatements significantly influence the tax

rate of the controlled community? Are abatements granted willingly by the local assessors or is the Appellate Tax Board involved? If rent control boards allow rent adjustments to compensate for property tax increases, do landlords still receive abatements?

5. *New residential construction.* How do construction rates in noncontrolled communities compare with those in controlled cities and towns? Will bankers give mortgages in rent-controlled communities? Does rent control prevent construction of new private multifamily dwelling units? How has Massachusetts construction fared in relation to nationwide averages? Has new construction of subsidized housing increased or decreased, in both controlled and noncontrolled communities?

6. *Maintenance of rental property.* Has rent control caused rental property to deteriorate or improve? Have landlords reduced maintenance as a response to regulated rent levels?

7. *Administrative costs and time lags for rent-control decisions.* How much does it cost for a community to administer rent control? How long does it take for rent control boards to decide on an individual petition? Has the time span between filing a petition and receiving a decision improved in communities that adopted rent control?

8. *Evictions.* How has Chapter 842 affected the eviction process?

Detailed Analysis

This study considered the statistical evidence in nearly every large city and town in the commonwealth. We researched Boston, Brookline, Cambridge, and Somerville in depth and Lynn to a somewhat lesser degree. In addition, we gathered statistical data pertaining to Arlington, Brockton, Chicopee, Fall River, Framingham, Lawrence, Lowell, Malden, Medford, New Bedford, Newton, Pittsfield, Quincy, Springfield, Waltham, Weymouth, and Worcester. Throughout Chapter 1, references in charts and tables to the rent-controlled communities relate to Boston, Brookline, Cambridge, Lynn (in most cases), and Somerville. References to the 17 noncontrolled cities and towns relate to the 17 large communities listed above.

Effectiveness of Rent Control in Controlling Rent

Table 1-1 displays the percentage increase in rent in four rent-controlled communities, the average rent increase between 1970 and 1974 for the controlled communities, and the consumer price index rent component for 1970 and 1974 in Boston.

Table 1-1
Estimated Rent Increases, 1970 to 1974

City/Town	Median Gross Rent, 1970[a]	Mean Rent, November, 1974	Percentage Increase, 1970-1974
Boston	$126	$145[d]	15.1%
Brookline	190	232[e]	22.1
Cambridge	134	160[f]	19.4
Somerville	128	139[g]	8.3
Average Rent in Controlled Communities[b]	131	152	16.0
Consumer Price Index, Rent Component for Boston[c]	113.5	144.9	27.6

[a]Data are from the 1970 U.S. Census of Housing. Median gross rent was used rather than contract rent, to make the 1970 and 1974 samples more consistent. The 1974 figures include rent-controlled units only (many of which include utilities in the rent), whereas the 1970 figures include all rental units (including the cost of utilities for all units).

[b]These rents were obtained by weighting the above figures by the estimated number of rent-controlled units in each municipality (Boston: 125,000; Brookline: 11,300; Cambridge: 20,424; Somerville: 10,000).

[c]The housing market area covered by the Bureau of Labor Statistics sample is roughly comparable to the Boston SMSA, including approximately 407,583 rental units. An estimated 44 percent of these units are now rent-controlled (180,913 units). However, 125,000 units in Boston were not covered by Chapter 842 until January, 1973. This index, therefore, is heavily influenced, during the period 1970-1974, by the rents in noncontrolled units.

[d]Based upon a sample of 9,758 rental units for which adjustment petitions were filed between March and August 1974. The figure as shown is biased on the high side since the sample reflects recent decisions.

[e]Derived from a sample of 346 units conducted by Harbridge House and an opinion poll of his staff conducted by Director-Counsel of Rent Control Board. Weighted by proportion of one-, two-, and three-bedroom units in the town (29 percent, 38 percent, and 18 percent respectively).

[f]Based upon a sample of rent-controlled units by the Cambridge Rent Control Board, in January 1974 (the best available estimate).

[g]Calculations by Urban Planning Aid demonstrate that the cumulative increase of all rent adjustments represented an 8.3 percent increase over 1970 levels. The 1970 census figure of $128 was then increased by 8.3 percent, yielding $139.

The data leads to the following conclusions:

1. The average rent in controlled communities increased 16.0 percent during the four-year period. These figures include the effect of inflation.
2. Simultaneously, the consumer price index rent component for Boston rose 27.6 percent, indicating the effect of inflation on rent in the greater Boston area.

3. Thus the effect of rent control was to keep rent approximately 28 percent lower than the average for the greater Boston area.

The Boston Rent Control Board has made available an analysis of 3,062 recent decisions affecting 29,615 dwelling units, yielding the following data:

1. 3,830 dwelling units were *denied* any increase in rent. The average monthly rent requested was $185.52; the actual average monthly rent remained at $163.95.
2. 6,494 dwelling units *neither requested nor received an increase in rent.* The average monthly rent was $165.86 for units in this group. (This group includes redistribution of rents within a structure.)
3. 8,714 dwelling units were granted the *full increase* requested. The average monthly rent before petitioning was $161.46; the average monthly rent after the decision was $175.72.
4. 10,577 dwelling units received *partial increases.* The average monthly rent before petitioning was $162.88; the average rent requested was $190.28; the average rent granted was $175.99.

The Boston Rent Control Board's record, therefore, in maintaining a steady average monthly rent is remarkable. Each case is considered individually; yet the result for petitions receiving the full requested increase is within $0.27 of the result for petitions receiving partial increases.

Vacancy Rates

The primary measures of the vacancy rate for rental units are (1) postal vacancy surveys, (2) U.S. Census, and (3) studies commissioned by special-interest groups to investigate limited market areas. The postal vacancy data is derived from reports by mailmen, and its conclusions are generally believed to be lower than the "true vacancy rate." A postman's observations concerning apartments depend too heavily upon false impressions. His report is affected by (a) whether he thinks a resident is on vacation or at home, (b) whether he thinks a newly constructed apartment is available for occupancy, (c) whether he thinks a substandard unit is clearly labeled "condemned" or is boarded-up, and (d) whether he thinks two units share one mailbox (e.g., a roomer-boarder subleasing part of a unit without obtaining a separate mailbox). The postal vacancy survey is taken by individuals with no consistent sampling method.

The U.S. Census figures also tend to be biased due to the observer's unfamiliarity with the status of each individual rental unit. The census considers an abandoned unit as vacant as long as there is no indication that the unit is unfit for occupancy. In addition, a newly constructed unit is recorded as available for habitation as soon as it offers protection from the elements. Thus the census vacancy figures tend to overestimate the number of available units.

Studies performed by nongovernment agencies draw contradictory conclusions. Some surveys rely on newspaper advertisements for vacancy data, although many highly desirable units are rented quickly without the benefit of such ads. Several studies project a vacancy figure from a sample, thus magnifying any biases inherent in the original sample.

A search for alternative methods of obtaining vacancy data proved unsuccessful. Telephone connections cannot yield data specifically for rental units, especially for units without telephones. Utility meters, such as electricity and fuel, are unreliable measures of vacancies because (1) the relationship between meters and residential units is not one-to-one (one meter may service the entire building), and (2) utility connections in rental units cannot be distinguished from other residential units.

Despite the lack of an accurate measure of vacancy rates, the numerous studies agree upon one trend, i.e., the rate is low enough to create a significant impact on the price of rental housing. (See Table 1-2.)

Rental Housing Association Vacancy and Market Surveys

The Rental Housing Association (RHA) conducts an annual survey of its members to determine current vacancy and market information. The survey, conducted by The Analytical Sciences Corporation (TASC), received responses concerning 22,880 units in 1971, and 30,368 units in 1972. All the figures in Table 1-3 were obtained directly from the RHA studies. However, RHA obtained its vacancy figures for 1970 from the 1970 U.S. Census Bureau reports on housing.

The RHA vacancy rates for 1971 and 1972, when compared with the 1970 U.S. Census figures, indicate an increase in the percentage of vacant rental units in the greater Boston area. Closer examination, however, reveals a 1972 vacancy rate of less than 5 percent for one-, three-, and four-bedroom units, which make up 80.4 percent of the total rental units in the greater Boston area, according to RHA surveys. The 1972 vacancy rate for units with a monthly rent under $125 was 4.1 percent. The rate for units renting for $125 to $159 was 5.3 percent. The sample sizes yielding the above vacancy figures were 3,119 and 4,051 units, respectively. Many of the units in the sample were obtained from landlords owning large structures, demonstrated by the fact that responses were received for 30,368 units in less than 1,100 buildings—an average of more than 27 units per structure.

Table 1-2
Apartment Vacancy Rate from Postal Vacancy Surveys
(Percent of Total Apartments Unoccupied)[a]

City/Town	CIRCA 1966	CIRCA 1970	CIRCA 1973
Arlington	0.7	0.2	2.6
Boston	2.8	1.9	3.5
Brookline	3.3	0.7	0.6
Cambridge	1.6	0.6	1.2
Chicopee	2.3	2.1	3.1
Framingham	3.5	0.1	3.4
Lynn	4.3	2.7	N/A
Malden	1.7	0.5	1.0
Medford	0.6	0.9	0.7
Newton	3.3	N/A[b]	1.1
Quincy	2.0	1.7	1.8
Somerville	1.6	N/A	0.8
Springfield	4.7	5.0	5.9
Waltham	4.9	N/A[b]	1.1
Weymouth	1.1	2.7	5.3
Worcester	N/A[b]	2.0	2.8

[a]Postal Vacancy Surveys were not conducted in any of the three years displayed above in Brockton, Fall River, Lawrence, Lowell, New Bedford, and Pittsfield. All available data from the Postal Surveys for the cities mentioned on this page have been presented above.
[b]N/A = Not Available.

Vacancy Rates in Cambridge

The results of a vacancy study conducted by the Cambridge Rent Control Board on November 28, 1973[1] indicate an overall vacancy rate of 0.48 percent in Cambridge. Further analysis reveals that 43 of the vacant units asked for monthly rent in excess of $200, representing 0.21 percent of all units and 44 percent of the 98 vacant units. Fifty-five of the vacant units asked for monthly rent less than $200, representing 0.27 percent of all units and 56 percent of the 98 vacant units.

Vacancy Rates—Postal Vacancy Survey Versus Housing Association Survey

A comparison between the postal vacancy data (obtained in April 1973) and the Rental Housing Association vacancy data (obtained in November 1972) follows.

Table 1-3
Rental Housing Association and Postal Vacancy Survey Data

City/Town	Rental Housing Association, November 1972 (%)	Postal Vacancy, April 1973 (%)	Difference (%)
Total Boston	5.7	3.5	+2.2
Back Bay	5.9	8.1	−2.2
Brighton	5.5	1.6	+3.9
Dorchester	8.8	3.0	+5.8
Hyde Park	9.2	5.5	+3.7
Roxbury	4.5	6.0	−1.5
West Roxbury	2.2	0.7	+1.5
Brookline	2.0	0.6	+1.4
Cambridge	1.6	1.2	+0.4
Framingham	2.0	3.4	−1.4
Quincy	2.4	1.8	+0.6
Stoneham	5.8	2.6	+3.2
Waltham	1.0	1.1	+0.1
Weymouth	7.0	5.3	+1.7

These surveys attempt to characterize essentially the same rental housing situation, since a five-month interval does not generally permit significant shifts in true vacancy rates.

Vacancies in Public Housing in Boston

The Boston Housing Authority provided us with vacancy statistics as of September 30, 1974 for subsidized housing. Four projects alone contribute 61 percent of the vacant units: Mission Hill, Mission Hill Extension, Columbia Point, and Franklin Field. These four projects experience high vacancy rates, as well as high vandalism rates; and increased vandalism inhibits the influx of tenants that would occur if these projects were located in more desirable sections of Boston. (See Table 1-4.)

The following conclusions are supported by the data:

1. Over half the vacant one-bedroom units are within the four projects currently experiencing high vandalism rates.
2. Six out of every ten vacant two-bedroom units are also in those four projects.
3. Three out of every four vacant three-bedroom units are within the four projects.
4. Nearly three out of every four vacant four-bedroom units are in the four projects.

Table 1-4
Vacant Units in Boston's Public Housing

Unit Size	Boston, Citywide	Total Number of Vacant Units For: Mission Hill, Mission Hill Extension, Columbia Point, Franklin Field Only	Boston Citywide, Excluding the Four Projects
Efficiency	36	0	36
One-bedroom	523	277	246
Two-bedroom	412	263	149
Three-bedroom	266	205	61
Four-bedroom	49	36	13
Five-bedroom	8	3	5
Six-bedroom	3	2	1
Total	1,297	786	511

Source: Boston Housing Authority.

The following conclusions are supported by the data:
1. Over half the vacant one-bedroom units are within the four projects currently experiencing high vandalism rates.
2. Six out of every ten vacant two-bedroom units are also in those four projects.
3. Three out of every four vacant three-bedroom units are within the four projects.
4. Nearly three out of every four vacant four-bedroom units are in the four projects.

Waiting Lists for Public Housing in 1970[2]

In 1968, some 14,000 people were on waiting lists for state-aided housing for the elderly and were considered eligible. Annual admissions totalled approximately 1,700; so an elderly person might expect to wait eight years, on the average, to enter. This delay discouraged many other people from applying. Also in 1968, there were approximately 6,000 families on waiting lists for state-aided housing. Since only 1,700 (approximately) are admitted annually, the waiting period was about three and a half years for most of the families.

In comparison, for federally-aided housing in 1968, a total of 11,400 elderly people were still on the waiting list in 1970 and only 1,000 were being admitted annually. This represented a waiting period of over 11 years for most of the people on the list. In contrast, the length of the waiting list for families was six years.

Current Waiting Lists for Public Housing in Rent-Controlled Communities

Based on statistics gathered by local housing authorities, the following waiting lists currently exist:

1. Cambridge notes 1,500 households on its list. Approximately 600 to 700 of those are elderly tenants. About 450 elderly people have been offered a unit but have refused it, in order to wait for a "better" unit.[3]
2. Somerville notes an estimated 500 families and 700 elderly households on its waiting lists.[4]

Vacancy Rates by Rent Ranges

Although the 1970 U.S. Census measure of vacancy rates in rental units is considered to overestimate the actual vacancy rate, it is useful to examine the census breakdown of vacant rental units by contract rent ranges,[5] i.e., payments by renters directly to the landlord. (These figures exclude one-family homes on ten or more acres.) The vacancy rates in the following tables were obtained by dividing the number of vacant rental units in each category by the sum of the number of occupied rental units plus vacant rental units. The calculations were performed separately for rental units with all plumbing facilities and for units lacking some or all plumbing facilities. The proportion of rental units in each community which falls in the latter category is shown in Table 1-5.

Vacancy Rates–Massachusetts Housing Finance Agency

We obtained from the management office of the Massachusetts Housing Finance Agency (MHFA) a survey of vacancy and tenant income conducted during September 1974. Several errors were found among the large volume of developments surveyed. However, the magnitude of error is relatively small.

We calculated the number of rented and vacant units broken down by rent ranges, the vacancy rates broken down by rent ranges, and the waiting lists broken down by rent ranges. We investigated four rent-controlled communities (Somerville does not have any MHFA developments) and seven noncontrolled communities (New Bedford and Worcester were excluded due to a large number of erroneous data). Four of the 17 noncontrolled communities investigated elsewhere in this study do not have MHFA financed housing at this time (Arlington, Chicopee, Malden, and Medford).

The data in Table 1-6 indicate a lower vacancy rate as well as a proportionately bigger waiting list in the rent-controlled communities (Boston, Brookline, Cambridge, and Lynn). These four communities provide a greater percentage of low-income families with housing than other urban communities with MHFA housing units provide. The long waiting lists for both rent-controlled and noncontrolled cities demonstrate the need in low- and moderate-income ranges for rental units. Moreover, the low-income units by far have the longest waiting lists.

Table 1-5
1970 U.S. Census Vacancy Rate for Rental Units by Rent Range

Monthly Rent Asked	Vacancy Rate of Units With All Plumbing Facilities (%)	Vacancy Rate of Units Lacking Some or All Plumbing Facilities (%)
Boston		
Less than $40	6.2	9.1
$40 to $59	7.9	10.9
$60 to $79	7.7	10.3
$80 to $99	5.5	10.0
$100 to $149	4.7	7.3
$150 or more	4.8	7.3
All Rent Ranges	5.7	9.8
Median Rent Asked	$91	N/A
Brookline		
Less than $40	4.7%	
$40 to $59	3.1	
$60 to $79	1.5	
$80 to $99	0	This category is too small to perform valid statistical analyses.
$100 to $149	1.4	
$150 or more	1.7	
All Rent Ranges	1.6%	
Median Rent Asked	$206	
Cambridge		
Less than $40	2.4%	2.7%
$40 to $59	2.7	8.6
$60 to $79	2.6	3.6
$80 to $99	2.4	4.1
$100 to $149	2.6	3.3
$150 or more	2.3	2.0
All Rent Ranges	2.4%	4.9%
Median Rent Asked	$119	N/A
Somerville		
Less than $40	1.0%	6.5%
$40 to $59	0.7	3.6
$60 to $79	2.2	3.6
$80 to $99	2.4	3.2
$100 to $149	2.4	0.7
$150 or more	3.3	0
All Rent Ranges	2.3%	3.2
Median Rent Asked	$101	N/A

N/A = Not available.

MHFA market rate units appear to be the most difficult to rent, primarily due to their relatively high rental rates in most cases. This characteristic strongly affects developments for the elderly, where potential residents may be living on pensions or fixed incomes. The location of MHFA units also greatly affects the rate at which units are occupied.

The developments which have unusually high vacancy rates are still frequently in the "rent-up stage," which may last as long as six to 12 months. The footnotes to Table 1-6 explain when vacancy rates are highly inflated due to one development still renting for the first time.

Income of Tenants in the Greater Boston Area

The most comprehensive and periodic indicator of tenant's income in the greater Boston area is the quarterly figures published by the Bureau of Labor Statistics.[6] The index is compiled in several ways of interest: (1) average pre-tax earnings of factory production workers in dollars, (2) those earnings in 1967 dollars (to eliminate the effects of inflation), (3) average after-tax earnings of factory production workers with three dependents, in current dollars, and (4) those earnings in 1967 dollars.

Table 1-7 illustrates the average weekly earnings of factory production workers in Boston from 1968 to 1974. The most recent publication indicates that in July 1974, a worker with three dependents brought home $156.82, on the average, after taxes. Compared to his 1967 earnings, he earned $2.38 more in 1974 (restated in 1967 dollars).

Clearly, gross average weekly earnings in 1974 have actually declined since 1973. If we consider gross weekly earnings restated in 1967 dollars, the average of the January, April, and July figures is $121.11—nearly $7 less per week than the average for 1973 (in 1967 dollars, $128.08). Even more significantly, net spendable earnings declined to a 1974 average to date of $103.84 in real (1967) dollars.

We assume that most low- and moderate-income tenants are experiencing effects on their income similar to those upon factory production workers. Thus we could expect a general decline of average weekly earnings in the Boston metropolitan area during 1974.

Rent and Landlords' Expenses in the Greater Boston Area

Several sources were considered in order to determine landlords' expenses and rent. Only one source—consumer price indices—was adequate for these purposes.

The consumer price index for each item (Table 1-8) reveals the percentage increase in cost over its 1967 price, stated in 1967 dollars. The effect of inflation is thus eliminated from our analysis.

Table 1-6
Massachusetts Housing Finance Agency Rental Statistics as of September 1974

City/Town	Occupied Units Market Rent	Occupied Units Moderate Rent	Occupied Units Low Rent	Vacant Units Market Rent	Vacant Units Moderate Rent	Vacant Units Low Rent	Total Occupied	Total Vacant	Vacancy Rates Market	Vacancy Rates Moderate	Vacancy Rates Low	Waiting List Market	Waiting List Moderate	Waiting List Low
Boston	535	813	746	94[a]	104[b]	29	2,094	227	15%[a]	11%[b]	4%	55	322	1,627
Brookline	147	146	101	0	0	0	394	0	0	0	0	N/A	45	N/A
Cambridge	122	168	263	67[c]	41[d]	18[e]	553	126	35[c]	19[d]	0[e]	16	110	54
Lynn	1	2	6	0	0	0	9	0	0	0	0	N/A	N/A	110
Brockton	43	341	147	47[f]	10	0	531	57	52[f]	3	0	28	249	407
Fall River	84	367	148	23[g]	5	0	599	28	21[g]	1	0	N/A	N/A	240
Framingham	47	95	48	4	0	0	190	4	8	0	0	N/A	12	41
Lawrence	35	–	34	1	–	1	69	2	3	–	3	18	N/A	45
Lowell	261	348	243	25[h]	2	1	852	28	9[h]	1	0	N/A	26	N/A
Springfield	–	158	69	–	7	0	227	7	–	4	0	N/A	10	125
Weymouth	124	64	63	7	0	0	251	7	5	0	0	N/A	20	260

N/A = Not available.

[a]Fifty-four of the vacant "market" units (representing over half of the 15 percent vacancy rate) are in Brighton, with a rental range of $325 to $355 for one-bedroom and $345 to $425 for two-bedroom units.

[b]Forty-two of the vacant "moderate" units (representing four tenths of the 11 percent vacancy rate) are in West Roxbury, which had been renting units for only 12 weeks at the time of this survey.

[c]Sixty-one of the vacant "market" units (representing almost all of the 35 vacancy rate) are at the Franklin Street Elderly development, which had been renting for only 12 weeks at the time of this survey.

[d]Twenty-three of the vacant "moderate" units (representing over half of the 19 vacancy rate) are at the Franklin Street Elderly development, which had been renting for only 12 weeks at the time of this survey.

[e]Fifteen of the vacant "low" units (representing nearly all of the 6 percent vacancy rate) are at the Franklin Street Elderly development, which had been renting for only 12 weeks at the time of this survey.

[f]All of the vacant "market" units (representing the entire 52 percent vacancy rate) are at one development, which had been renting for 20 weeks. Forty-five of the 47 units are one-bedroom units renting at $224 per month.

[g]Eighteen of the vacant "market" units (representing four fifths of the 21 percent vacancy rate) are at one development. This development had 100 percent occupancy of its low- and moderate-units at the time of this survey, but more than half of its market units were vacant. Rental rates are $219 for one-bedroom units and $256 for two-bedroom units per month.

[h]Twenty of the vacant "market" units (representing four fifths of the 9 percent vacancy rate) are at one development. Most of these vacant units were two-bedroom units renting at $245 to $250 per month. The low- and moderate-units in this development were at nearly 100 percent occupancy, however.

Table 1-7
Weekly Earnings of Factory Production Workers in Boston

	Year	Gross Average Weekly Earnings		Spendable Average Weekly Earnings (for Worker with Three Dependents)	
		Current	1967	Current	1967
Average	1967	$116.11	$116.11	$102.24	$102.24
Average	1968	122.19	117.38	106.50	102.31
Average	1969	128.51	116.83	110.67	100.61
Average	1970	137.94	118.20	119.25	102.19
Average	1971	147.38	120.11	128.08	104.38
Average	1972	160.00	125.89	139.69	109.91
Average	1973	172.53	128.08	148.23	110.04
January	1974	174.99	123.23	150.15	105.74
April	1974	170.94	117.65	146.99	101.16
July	1974	183.54	122.44	156.82	104.62

Source: 1967-1973 data obtained directly from U.S. Department of Labor. 1974 data obtained from the Bureau of Labor Statistics "Net Spendable Earnings in Boston: July 1974," BO-1-74-08-29-245, released October 1974.

Although tenants' real income has declined during 1974, rents in the greater Boston area have risen. The increased rents reflect the skyrocketing costs of fuel oil, coal, gas, electricity, household furnishings, and general operations. The largest increases were in utilities (a 43 percent rise over its 1973 average). Utilities generally represent only 6 to 8 percent of rent. Meanwhile, rents have risen only 6.4 percent in comparison to the 1973 average.

An additional trend relevant to our study is suggested by the consumer price index homeownership component. In every year since 1968, the cost to the consumer of buying a home has risen more rapidly than has the cost of residential rent. The implication of this trend is that renter-households find it increasingly difficult to leave the rental market as the gap widens between the two components. The rental housing shortage is therefore intensified.

Rise in Rents Versus Rise in Tenants' Income

Several sources were investigated to develop a comparison between the increase in rents and the increase in tenants' income (i.e., wages) over a period of time. The source offering the least time-consuming comparison was the U.S. Census. Tables 1-9 and 1-10 and Figure 1-1 illustrate the median gross rent per month, 1960 and 1970; the median family income, 1959 and 1969; and the percent increase in median income and median rent between 1960 and 1970.

Table 1-8
Consumer Price Index for Urban Wage Earners and Clerical Workers in the Boston Metropolitan Area (1967 = 100)

	Average 1968	Average 1969	Average 1970	Average 1971	Average 1972	Average 1973	January 1974	April 1974	July 1974	October 1974	United States Mean Index Through October 1974[a]
Rent (Residential)	102.7	108.8	115.4	122.7	129.2	136.2	140.2	141.3	143.0	144.9	132.2
Homeownership	106.1	116.3	128.3	138.1	147.6	153.1	160.4	159.1	163.6	165.3	170.1
Fuel Oil and Coal	101.4	102.3	108.5	114.9	117.1	137.9	187.1	195.9	214.9	221.2	225.5
Gas and Electricity	100.3	101.3	105.6	115.9	120.8	126.5	138.4	149.6	146.7	157.8	151.5
Household Furnishings and Operation	106.2	111.8	117.3	123.0	125.8	130.5	134.8	139.7	155.6	152.7	149.0
Consumer Price Index for all Items—Boston	104.1	110.0	116.7	122.7	127.1	134.7	142.0	145.2	149.7	153.0	146.3

[a] Average of quarterly figures, or monthly figures when available.
Source: U.S. Department of Labor, Bureau of Labor Statistics.

Table 1-9
Median Gross Rent per Month

City/Town	1960	1970	Percent Increase 1960-1970
Arlington	$107	$168	57
Boston	78	126	62
Brockton	67	107	60
Brookline	121	190	57
Cambridge	79	134	70
Chicopee	71	96	35
Fall River	55	83	51
Framingham	85	153	80
Lawrence	65	96	48
Lowell	63	106	68
Lynn	78	112	44
Malden	83	124	49
Medford	89	133	49
New Bedford	59	86	46
Newton	108	175	62
Pittsfield	73	106	45
Quincy	86	132	53
Somerville	83	128	54
Springfield	73	100	37
Waltham	92	144	57
Weymouth	84	151	80
Worcester	70	104	49
All Massachusetts	75	90	20

Source: U.S. Department of Commerce, Bureau of the Census, 1960 and 1970.

The following comparisons and conclusions are apparent:

1. Five cities experienced percentage increases in median rent which surpassed percentage increases in median family income: Boston, Cambridge, Framingham, Lowell, and Weymouth.

2. The average increase in median gross monthly rent from 1960 to 1970 for the five rent-controlled communities was 57 percent; for the 17 noncontrolled communities it was 54 percent; and for the entire Commonwealth of Massachusetts it was 20 percent.

3. The communities which subsequently adopted Chapter 842, therefore, experienced a slightly higher rate of increase in median rent than the other communities considered here. Both groups experienced rates of increase in rents well over the statewide average.

Table 1-10
Median Family Income, 1959 and 1969

City/Town	1959	1969	Percent Increase, 1959-1969
Arlington	$6,989	$12,247	75
Boston	5,747	9,133	59
Brockton	5,914	10,377	75
Brookline	8,164	13,701	68
Cambridge	5,923	9,815	66
Chicopee	6,170	9,738	58
Fall River	4,970	8,289	67
Framingham	7,478	13,090	75
Lawrence	5,508	9,507	73
Lowell	5,679	9,495	67
Lynn	6,021	9,739	62
Malden	6,194	10,204	65
Medford	6,693	11,145	67
New Bedford	5,019	8,230	64
Newton	9,008	15,381	71
Pittsfield	6,455	10,678	65
Quincy	6,785	11,094	64
Somerville	6,024	9,594	59
Springfield	5,994	9,612	60
Waltham	6,804	11,523	69
Weymouth	6,667	11,631	74
Worcester	5,804	10,038	73
All Massachusetts	6,272	10,835	73

Source: U.S. Department of Commerce, Bureau of the Census, 1960 and 1970.

4. Median family income rose an average of 73 percent in Massachusetts. For rent-controlled communities, the average increase was 63 percent. Thus median family income rose more quickly statewide than it did in the 17 noncontrolled cities and towns with more than 55,000 inhabitants. Median family income rose even more slowly in the five rent-controlled communities.

The median gross rent figure obtained from the U.S. Census is most likely much lower than the average gross rent paid. The census data includes tenants in public and other subsidized housing in its sample; these tenants often pay as much as $100 below market rates per month. The median gross rent paid by tenants in nonsubsidized housing was actually higher, therefore, than the figures in Table 1-9 indicate.

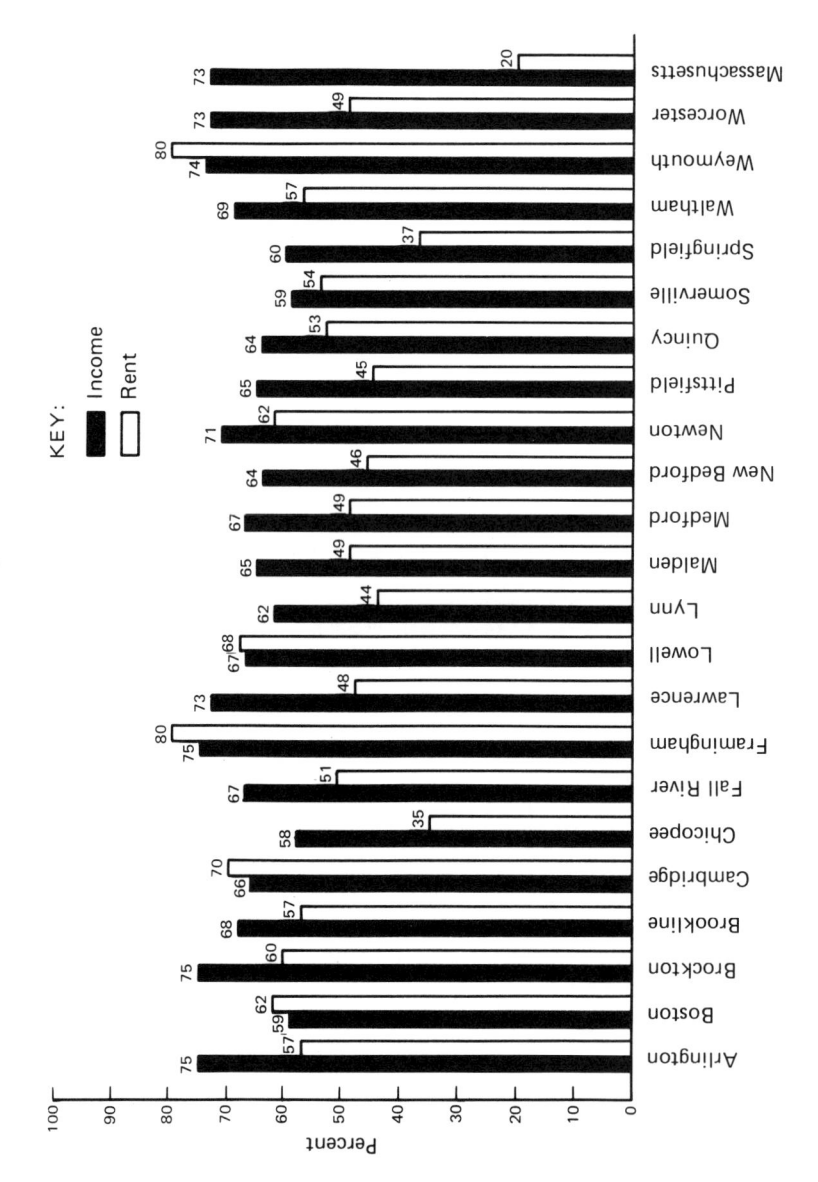

Figure 1-1. Percent Increase in Median Income and Median Rent Between 1960 and 1970 (Based on U.S. Census Figures) by City or Town.

Brookline-Relationship Between Cash Expenditures
of Landlords and Gross Revenue, Assessed Value, Etc.

Mr. Joseph Eckert, professor of economics at Curry College and a member of the Brookline Rent Control Board, has conducted detailed analyses of Brookline data. His analysis of key expenses as a percentage of rent, net operating income as a percentage of rent, and profit as a percentage of assessed value yields the following conclusions:

1. Maintenance as a percentage of rent increased in Brookline between 1970 and 1972. The 1972 figure was 4.5 percent versus 3.9 and 3.4 in prior years. This conclusion is contrary to the argument expressed by many landlords and real estate management agencies that rent control causes decreased maintenance of rental housing.

2. No pattern is discernible concerning higher maintenance as a percentage of rent in one type of dwelling structure versus another. Structures with one to ten units are just as likely to spend a greater proportion of rent on maintenance as are buildings with 11 to 20 units or more than 20 units.

3. Property tax as a percentage of rent was greatest for structures with one to ten units in 1970 and 1971. In 1972, however, property tax as a percentage of rent was higher for buildings with more than 20 units. For all rental units taken together, however, property tax represented less than 30 percent of gross rent in all three years under consideration. This finding is contrary to the argument that rent control has forced property owners to assume the burden of increased taxation alone. As additional studies by Mr. Eckert demonstrate (see pages 27 and 28 concerning abatements of property taxes on rent-controlled units), the effect of abatements due to taxes being greater than 30 percent of gross income is negligible.

4. Cash expenditures as a percentage of rent was approximately 59 percent in 1970 and 1971 and rose to 62 percent in 1972. Unfortunately, the 1973 and 1974 figures are not available for this item.

5. Net operating income as a percentage of gross revenue declined from 40.5 percent in 1970 to 39.9 percent in 1971 and to 37.6 percent in 1972. Consistently, the type of structure that obtained the greatest profit in relation to gross revenue was the building with more than 20 units. The data for this category indicates an initial 41.4 percent in 1970, an increase to 43.4 percent in 1971 (while profits to revenue dropped for the other two categories), and a subsequent decline to 39.8 percent in 1972.

6. Few patterns can be discerned concerning profit as a percentage of assessed valuation. The mean for all sizes of structures was 9 percent in 1970; it rose to 10.5 percent in 1971; and it decreased to 9.6 percent in 1972. The dwellings with 11 to 20 units earned the lowest profit in relation to the assessed value of all types of structures in all three years. Table 1-11 illustrates Mr. Eckert's results.

Table 1-11
Maintenance, Property Taxes, Total Expenses, and Net Operating Income as a Percentage of Rent; Profit as a Percentage of Valuation

	Mean, 1970	Standard Deviation	Mean, 1971	Standard Deviation	Mean, 1972	Standard Deviation
Maintenance as Percentage of Rent						
1 to 10 Units	3.6%	4.2%	3.4%	4.2%	5.1%	5.4%
11 to 20 Units	3.7	2.8	3.6	2.2	4.0	4.0
More than 20 Units	4.3	3.7	3.2	3.0	4.5	2.0
Total	3.9%	3.6%	3.4%	3.1%	4.5%	3.8%
Property Tax as Percentage of Rent						
1 to 10 Units	29.0%	8.3%	29.9%	9.0%	29.4%	8.1%
11 to 20 Units	26.1	4.8	26.0	3.3	28.9	2.4
More than 20 Units	27.1	4.4	25.5	2.8	30.4	3.4
Total	27.4%	5.8%	27.1%	5.0%	29.6%	4.6%
Cash Expenditures as Percentage of Rent						
1 to 10 Units	60.0%	11.5%	62.1%	12.2%	62.7%	9.3%
11 to 20 Units	59.9	8.7	61.5	7.7	64.5	4.7
More than 20 Units	57.4	11.9	54.1	8.6	60.1	8.7
Total	59.1%	10.7%	59.2%	9.5%	62.4%	7.6%
Net Operating Income as Percentage of Gross Revenue						
1 to 10 Units	40.0%	11.6%	37.9%	12.3%	37.5%	9.5%
11 to 20 Units	40.0	8.8	38.4	7.7	35.5	4.0
More than 20 Units	41.4	11.6	43.4	13.1	39.8	8.7
Total	40.5%	10.7%	39.9%	11.0%	37.6%	7.4%
Profit as Percentage of Assessed Valuation						
1 to 10 Units	9.3%	7.0%	10.0%	9.1%	10.7%	10.0%
11 to 20 Units	8.8	2.6	9.7	1.9	8.4	1.1
More than 20 Units	9.0	2.9	11.7	3.2	9.8	2.8
Total	9.0%	4.2%	10.5%	4.7%	9.6%	4.6%

Note: These data represent cash flow expenses for landlords. For example, the figures do not include depreciation. All figures have been transformed to eliminate the effects of inflation. Hence one *cannot* explain changes in the data by the effects of inflation. The term *maintenance* refers to upkeep and minor repairs. It does not include major capital expenditures.

Property Valuations

Opponents of rent control claim that property values go down if rents are controlled. The assessed valuation of property is based on the capitalization of income approach. If rents are fixed, then property values do not rise as they ordinarily would according to this argument. Market prices do not increase and may decrease. Opponents of rent control point to cities such as Cambridge and Lynn as examples.

We find that in Cambridge, the total assessed valuation of property has increased every year from 1968 until 1973. The city of Lynn experienced a decreasing property valuation in 1969, 1970, 1971, and 1973; rent control was enacted during the decline. A similar situation occurred in Somerville where the total assessed valuation of real estate consistently declined from 1968 to 1973 (except in 1970).

However, a change in the total assessed valuation of a city or town does not necessarily reflect any change in the tax base. The total property valuation varies highly with fluctuations in the assessment ratio (for example, see Weymouth real estate, 1968 and 1969, when the assessment ratio changed from 35 percent in 1968 to 91 percent in 1969). If all property were assessed at full market value, then "equalized valuation" for Cambridge property would be $838 million in 1974, a 61 percent increase over the 1972 figure.

The impact of rent control as the primary cause of declining property valuation cannot be determined. The rent-controlled cities experienced increasing equalized property values for several years prior to the inception of rent control. Table 1-12 indicates personal and real taxable property valuations for 1968-1973.

If a large proportion of property in a municipality is tax-exempt, then a greater proportion of tax is borne by the taxable properties. Some tax-exempt institutions contribute payments in lieu of taxes. However, these payments do not significantly offset the loss in revenue to the city or town due to exemptions. The cities which have a substantial amount of tax-exempt, real estate property are Boston (59 percent), Cambridge (49 percent), Medford (48 percent), and Lowell (39 percent). (See Tables 1-13 and 1-14.)

Tax Rates: Rent-Controlled Versus Noncontrolled Communities

The different assessment ratios that each community uses make it difficult to analyze changes in tax rates without some transformation of the data. Table 1-15 displays the estimated tax rate of 22 communities, assuming that each one assessed its property at 100 percent valuation. Our analysis focused on the tax rates for the years 1970-1973.

Table 1-12
Real Estate and Personal Property Valuations, 1968 to 1973

City/Town	1968 Personal	1968 Real Estate	1969 Personal	1969 Real Estate	1970 Personal	1970 Real Estate
Arlington	$ 6,438,300	$ 91,879,300	$ 10,687,300	$ 333,345,160	$ 11,184,600	$ 334,342,700
Boston	148,048,700	1,424,259,300	152,268,200	1,446,731,800	157,081,400	1,459,918,600
Brockton	11,408,200	142,018,150	11,838,300	145,778,300	12,409,700	151,992,750
Brookline	19,418,600	412,418,600	20,011,200	419,744,500	19,830,700	424,511,200
Cambridge	33,186,700	270,304,500	34,114,000	278,546,200	36,284,500	279,799,900
Chicopee	6,820,600	82,029,460	7,863,650	84,326,970	7,054,200	87,415,770
Fall River	14,817,450	111,477,550	15,118,700	110,761,950	15,222,450	112,349,050
Framingham	16,988,700	320,669,700	23,743,800	403,252,300	22,949,645	425,461,918
Lawrence	10,679,500	88,974,000	10,664,200	89,542,200	11,048,200	91,249,600
Lowell	13,543,900	133,474,700	18,620,700	136,747,900	14,016,550	140,083,000
Lynn	16,099,216	132,819,275	14,209,760	131,049,950	13,649,760	129,795,125
Malden	11,149,850	98,848,800	11,227,800	100,555,700	11,672,750	102,058,900
Medford	8,347,100	113,135,900	8,395,500	115,414,050	8,736,700	116,010,550
New Bedford	25,355,325	137,453,975	25,412,550	138,404,000	25,823,050	141,067,250
Newton	20,257,250	312,951,050	21,489,600	318,600,150	22,180,650	324,760,550
Pittsfield	15,050,210	261,182,500	15,216,100	268,013,400	21,388,020	272,626,200
Quincy	13,313,200	181,166,125	13,697,725	192,069,950	14,586,225	195,847,025
Somerville	12,110,400	124,371,000	12,452,700	123,968,500	13,467,000	124,430,100
Springfield	51,427,180	530,800,980	54,674,380	545,580,390	60,398,260	556,185,840
Waltham	14,161,114	142,521,720	14,220,749	145,727,801	14,558,649	149,517,790
Weymouth	33,263,825	115,299,800	44,901,700	305,616,100	47,040,800	307,717,550
Worcester	34,755,150	355,644,900	36,048,600	359,409,800	37,308,650	368,333,250

Source: Annual Recapitulation Sheets for Each Municipality Filed With Massachusetts Department of Corporations and Taxation, Bureau of Local Taxation.

City/Town	1971 Personal	1971 Real Estate	1972 Personal	1972 Real Estate	1973 Personal	1973 Real Estate
Arlington	$ 10,958,550	$ 337,440,550	$ 11,163,150	$ 339,254,700	$ 11,708,350	$ 341,960,750
Boston	179,190,000	1,502,310,000	183,838,200	1,531,861,800	207,493,300	1,534,706,700
Brockton	12,760,200	158,228,850	13,876,900	166,457,600	15,401,300	170,823,050
Brookline	21,504,400	425,082,800	18,737,400	426,064,800	19,288,800	428,563,700
Cambridge	38,994,100	280,701,900	43,679,500	281,758,900	49,050,800	277,001,700
Chicopee	7,441,990	88,491,070	7,569,240	89,380,700	7,602,000	91,336,510
Fall River	15,628,150	113,329,950	18,972,000	136,197,750	18,965,700	138,134,300
Framingham	23,812,962	442,435,855	24,981,550	460,130,351	27,684,024	492,992,850
Lawrence	12,011,700	92,682,400	12,585,700	96,427,700	13,882,600	100,463,000
Lowell	14,428,650	143,633,250	15,338,200	145,348,700	16,362,800	145,199,350
Lynn	15,426,100	126,982,330	15,539,850	134,916,270	11,944,833	131,269,530
Malden	12,633,950	102,279,050	13,284,900	103,123,750	13,626,200	104,774,050
Medford	8,778,700	116,305,150	9,148,950	116,425,550	9,530,150	121,647,950
New Bedford	26,768,350	142,841,700	33,914,825	182,529,700	34,492,800	182,383,825
Newton	21,838,150	328,208,700	22,870,950	332,484,950	24,505,300	337,433,300
Pittsfield	26,725,190	276,674,350	25,697,885	278,520,200	27,775,945	281,223,850
Quincy	16,831,400	204,650,715	18,364,550	222,644,975	21,404,175	229,277,030
Somerville	14,144,700	124,243,600	14,716,300	123,433,450	16,112,150	122,809,150
Springfield	63,776,730	568,036,460	65,369,240	582,872,410	67,358,640	588,674,130
Waltham	23,997,000	464,774,281	24,300,800	456,859,800	24,320,950	466,334,450
Weymouth	48,308,450	316,113,150	49,444,650	324,468,800	50,227,250	337,681,100
Worcester	38,575,400	374,438,500	41,678,000	381,540,050	42,730,650	391,754,850

Table 1-13
Percentage of Real Estate Property by Valuation Which is Tax Exempt

City/Town	Percentage	City/Town	Percentage
Arlington	13	Malden	22
Boston	59	Medford	48
Brockton	37	New Bedford	34
Brookline	19	Newton	28
Cambridge	49	Pittsfield	28
Chicopee	25	Quincy	24
Fall River	35	Somerville	28
Framingham	18	Springfield	27
Lawrence	23	Waltham	24
Lowell	39	Weymouth	14
Lynn	27	Worcester	39

Source: Figures based upon 1973 data filed by each municipality with the Massachusetts Department of Corporation and Taxation.

The average increase in the full value tax rate for all 22 municipalities between 1970 and 1973 was 19.17 percent. The average increase for the 17 noncontrolled cities and towns was 17.78 percent. For the five controlled cities, the average increase was 23.94 percent. If we exclude Boston,[a] however (which experienced a 61 percent rise in its full value tax rate), we find that rent-controlled cities showed an 11.74 percent increase.

We find no statistical support for the argument that rent control causes the tax rate to rise more quickly. The evidence clearly demonstrates that the full value tax rate rose more *slowly* in four out of five of the rent-controlled communities. The analysis of actual tax rates is spurious, however, since so many variables cause the tax rate to change. The influence of an election year, for example, may cause the tax rate to drop temporarily. The Cherry Sheet reimbursements also motivate municipalities to vary tax rates.

Abatements Granted to Real Estate

The issue of abatements granted to rent-controlled properties is often cited as a factor adversely affecting the property tax structure. Opponents of rent control claim that the tax burden is shifted to single- and two-family homeowners to compensate for the abatements to rental properties. Evidence presented later in

---
[a]Boston's assessment ratio was 84 percent in 1969, 65 percent in 1970, and 81 percent in 1971. See the footnote to Table 1-15. Chapter 842 was not officially adopted in Boston until 1973, so the tax rate prior to 1973 does not reflect the effect of rent control.

Table 1-14
Valuation of Tax-Exempt Real Estate Property, 1973

City/Town	United States	United States Housing	Commonwealth of Massachusetts	City or Town	Literary Institutions	Benevolent Institutions	Charitable Institutions	Total Value of Tax Exempt Property
Arlington	$ 420,950	$ 6,024,500	$ 2,628,850	$ 29,124,150	$ 2,433,050	$ 316,300	$ 3,607,250	$ 51,522,100
Boston	109,033,600	111,148,800	567,583,300	838,620,200	216,985,300	173,820,500	72,009,000	2,165,178,200
Brockton	17,407,350	13,797,450	4,500,800	38,288,100	4,693,600	8,219,750	3,792,700	98,549,000
Brookline	390,000	8,672,000	2,165,700	42,988,700	27,912,300	1,492,500	4,799,600	98,805,800
Cambridge	570,100	16,461,400	11,679,100	34,453,300	126,769,400	1,154,500	20,946,400	266,034,600
Chicopee	4,173,710	–	170,000	18,451,370	4,996,750	–	34,130	29,960,840
Fall River	966,950	17,096,300	2,953,600	18,222,050	8,749,250	–	13,997,890	73,754,740
Framingham	222,750	6,373,700	25,776,600	43,037,604	11,592,040	6,547,600	3,751,900	106,136,884
Lawrence	310,400	1,307,100	322,700	13,311,700	2,988,700	–	7,016,200	29,885,100
Lowell	509,550	–	25,903,150	29,443,650	2,680,200	877,550	24,906,450	93,165,550
Lynn	987,000	6,867,075	574,425	25,683,445	2,188,675	–	4,788,400	47,519,520
Malden	120,000	7,092,700	168,100	10,948,410	2,349,350	257,800	3,734,050	29,957,760
Medford	466,650	14,901,600	12,131,400	47,058,450	23,509,532	6,644,840	1,746,700	114,128,122
New Bedford	2,920,600	15,871,525	4,177,650	41,773,950	3,915,325	13,358,975	3,318,525	93,145,050
Newton	48,000	1,676,500	960,400	51,939,550	51,758,250	5,390,450	1,971,350	128,090,500
Pittsfield	11,509,850	3,653,350	10,307,950	44,538,060	8,117,250	–	18,783,550	108,921,110
Quincy	1,878,825	6,556,850	8,248,650	42,035,320	5,110,850	–	992,700	71,655,170
Somerville	166,600	10,882,317	4,801,150	18,361,700	7,953,400	1,286,900	532,800	48,555,511
Springfield	6,545,270	26,657,638	4,172,190	75,034,753	36,491,595	17,196,110	25,772,620	214,417,896
Waltham	6,663,400	6,038,860	24,217,625	31,408,800	51,869,350	1,003,850	10,857,075	147,016,410
Weymouth	10,616,250	3,364,500	256,450	27,098,800	2,163,500	5,331,650	–	56,995,350
Worcester	1,702,400	20,653,500	34,792,500	68,433,650	57,714,750	39,042,000	7,204,500	253,549,150

Table 1-15
Estimated Full Value Tax Rate (if Assessment Ratio = 100%)

City/Town	1968 Estimated Full Value	1969 Estimated Full Value	1970 Estimated Full Value	1971 Estimated Full Value	1972 Estimated Full Value	1973 Estimated Full Value
Arlington	$ 36.80	$ 41.00	$ 47.40	$ 50.80	$ 52.30	$ 52.80
Boston	106.90	121.50	101.40[a]	141.50	161.30	163.30
Brockton	58.50	62.50	75.90	87.70	96.20	95.40
Brookline	35.90	43.30	58.30	62.90	62.20	63.50
Cambridge	50.30	58.00	69.20	83.40	92.40	94.40
Chicopee	41.00	48.50	50.50	55.60	53.60	53.40
Fall River	62.40	66.20	69.10	78.10	85.40	86.40
Framingham	44.00	38.00	43.00	49.50	49.40	51.00
Lawrence	41.10	45.20	56.10	63.10	66.80	68.60
Lowell	56.90	63.00	72.40	74.60	75.50	73.70
Lynn	40.30	45.40	58.40	60.00	75.00	68.70
Malden	56.70	62.10	65.10	76.00	83.00	77.40
Medford	42.90	52.80	57.60	70.00	68.40	66.80
New Bedford	52.50	53.30	61.30	71.90	76.40	75.90
Newton	44.30	50.00	58.20	62.00	72.60	71.30
Pittsfield	47.70	49.50	49.40	49.70	51.90	57.90
Quincy	44.90	55.90	53.30	62.70	73.00	75.60
Somerville	59.00	64.30	75.30	78.00	76.40	72.10
Springfield	54.50	57.80	63.70	68.20	72.30	73.80
Waltham	36.00	40.30	44.40	42.50	41.50	39.40
Weymouth	28.00	34.10	43.00	45.60	52.00	52.80
Worcester	66.30	80.50	76.40	85.80	89.80	94.90

[a]In Boston, the assessment ratio was 84 percent in 1969, 65 percent in 1970, and 81 percent in 1971. The ratio was lowered in 1970 for reasons independent of rent control. One can speculate that it was lowered because 1970 was an election year.
Source: Massachusetts Taxpayers Foundation.

this section indicates a contrary conclusion for Brookline. Preliminary data for Cambridge, which employs a "tax pass-through" formula, different from the other rent-controlled cities, lends support to the above claim. Abatement statistics for Cambridge are often used in an attempt to support the above claim; these statistics must be looked at especially closely since early rent increases in Cambridge were nullified by court action.

Abatements—Brookline

A detailed analysis of the impact of rent control upon abatements in Brookline was conducted by Professor Joseph Eckert, currently a member of the Brookline

Rent Control Board. The analysis of abatements from 1970 through 1972 was a response to Brookline Selectmen's questions concerning the impact of rent control on Brookline housing.

According to Joseph Eckert, the Ryan data displayed in Table 1-16 show that "the number of abatements of all types in all property classifications for 1970-1972" has fallen. In addition, the dollar amounts for multiapartments under rent control have also fallen. The possible shifting that could have occurred if the total abated amount was shifted to other property classifications would have resulted in a $.60 shift in 1970, a $.57 shift in 1971, and a $.40 shift in 1972. This is an insignificant amount and, in addition, only 1971 and 1972 were rent-control years.[7]

The second set of data, displayed in Table 1-17, was derived from the Official Abatement Record of the Town of Brookline to the Commonwealth of Massachusetts as reported on Form 150. The analysis was conducted by the Revenue and Rent Control Study Committee. The data do not include actions of the Appellate Tax Board, which accounts for the discrepancy between the Ryan data and Form 150 data. (The gross number totals in Form 150 tables are larger because the Ryan data excludes commercial property and multiapartment units not covered by rent control.)

Mr. Eckert notes in his memo that the Form 150 figures reflect a decreasing trend in both the number of abatements and the dollar amounts. "Abated dollars for rent-controlled properties with adjustments" increased in 1971 and 1972; however, the impact upon Brookline's tax rate is negligible ($.10 in 1971 and $.12 in 1972).

Table 1-16
Assessor's Data[a]

Year	Number of Abatements				Totals
	Single Family	Two-Family	Three-Family	Multifamily	
1970	79	17	7	107	205
1971	78	19	19	139	255
1972	69	13	6	96	184

Year	Dollars of Abatement Given for Multifamily Under Rent Control	Impact on Tax Rate	Amount of Abatements to Multifamily as Result of Appellate Tax Board Action or Threat of Action
1970	$307,068	$.60	$92,579
1971	257,846	.57	49,221
1972	182,679	.40	27,529

[a]Data compiled by Assessor Ryan for Revenue and Rent Control Study Committee, August 1973. Data excludes commercial properties and units exempt from rent control.
Source: Eckert memo to Brookline Revenue and Rent Control Study Committee.

Table 1-17
Eckert's Analysis of Form 150 Data (Official Abatement Record of Town of Brookline)

Year	Abated Dollars for All Types of Property	Impact on Tax Rate	Abated Dollars for Rent-Controlled Properties	Impact on Tax Rate	Abated Dollars for Rent-Controlled Properties with Adjustments	Impact on Tax Rate
1970	$703,366	$1.50	$240,660	$.53	$32,686	$.07
1971	396,359	.75	216,662	.48	46,768	.10
1972	222,558	.49	131,544	.92	54,912	.12

Source: Eckert memo to Brookline Revenue and Rent Control Study Committee.

Clearly, the rent-controlled properties which received both an adjustment and an abatement had less impact on the tax rate than rental properties that did not receive an adjustment. The latter group of rental properties did not seek adjustments, but received abatements instead. Mr. Eckert stated that his conclusions may be extended to any rent-controlled community which allows "pass through" of property taxes to the tenants similar to Brookline's method.

Abatements–Cambridge

Data obtained from the Cambridge Assessors' Office (Table 1-18) indicate that total abatements rose from 1970 to 1972, then dropped in 1973; the figures include statutory exemptions as well. We have obtained information concerning statutory exemptions for 1970-1973; Table 1-18 shows the calculations for total abatements minus statutory exemptions, yielding "valuation abatements."

According to Cambridge Assessor, Charles R. Laverty, Jr., "approximately $600,000 (out of $1,260,091) is for abatements in rent-controlled units" in 1973.[8] No systematic analysis has been made to verify this figure. Many of the

Table 1-18
Cambridge–Total Abatements (November 1974 Data)

Year	Total Abatements	Statutory Exemptions	Valuation Abatements
1970	$1,109,184	$496,861	$ 612,323
1971	1,726,428	629,959	1,096,469
1972	2,113,204	729,724	1,383,480
1973	2,002,353	742,262	1,260,091

rental properties to which Mr. Laverty is referring may have been penalized by nullification of rent increases, or the landlords may never have applied for a rent increase to which they were legitimately entitled.

Since 1972, the Cambridge Assessors' Office has settled with property owners, avoiding court action, by granting an abatement if property tax is in excess of 30 percent of gross income. The current procedure to use 30 percent as the cutoff point, based on 1972 settlements between 26 and 30 percent, was determined by the Appellate Tax Board. Mr. Laverty suggests that "an increase in rents to offset the increased taxes would eliminate the vast majority of these cases."

The Role of the Appellate Tax Board

Critics of rent control have argued that rent control destroys the property tax structure. If rent control limits rent increases to the amount of the tax increase, then in time taxes will represent a greater percentage of rent. The property owner whose taxes represent more than 30 percent of his gross revenue usually receives an abatement, either (1) through the local assessing department, or (2) (failing the first route) by appealing to the Massachusetts Appellate Tax Board (ATB).

Mr. Daniel McLean, Chairman of the ATB, disputes the contention of ATB's critics that it assists in undermining the tax structure of a rent-controlled community. In fact, according to Mr. McLean, the vast majority of rental property abatements in the rent-controlled cities and towns were granted at the local level, i.e., "settled out of court" prior to a decision by the ATB.

Our investigation confirms Mr. McLean's latter point that most cases recently before the ATB involving rental properties are settled prior to ATB action. However, his statements require a more detailed analysis. Since the inception of rent control, the ATB has usually decided in favor of landlords seeking abatements whose property taxes represented more than 26 to 30 percent of gross revenue. Local assessors, well aware of the legal expense and time involved defending an ATB case, observed this pattern. It proved less costly for the local assessor to automatically settle any case similar to those decided by the ATB in favor of the landlord. Cambridge assessors, for example, settle at 30 percent of gross income.

Do Banks Give Mortgages in Rent-Controlled Communities?

Many landlords and real-estate developers claim that they cannot obtain loans at the present time for construction of new apartment buildings in rent-controlled areas. A survey of Boston bankers, primarily chief loan officers, revealed several schools of thought:

Refusal to Grant Loans in a Rent-Controlled Community. Many thrift institutions and insurance companies refuse to make loans in rent-controlled municipalities. One banker suggested that out of state lending institutions are avoiding investment in any state which has enabling legislation for rent control.

The belief of this theory's proponents is that rent control limits the ability of the mortgagor to pay back the loan. The bankers fear changes in the enabling legislation that would place new construction under rent control, thus constricting the property owner's income. However, a loan underwriter, embracing the above argument, will not hesitate to underwrite a construction loan in a rent-controlled city if it seems to be a profitable investment.

Willing to Lend in a Controlled Community. One banker prefaced his argument by noting that his bank had no loan money at all at the present time. He indicated, however, that his portfolio included many loans in Boston, Brookline, and Cambridge which were underwritten regardless of rent control's influences. He felt that even if new construction comes under control within the next five to seven years, his bank will have already made a decent return on its investment.

Refusal to Grant Mortgages to Multifamily Dwellings Anywhere. Many bankers are not underwriting loans for apartment buildings in any city, simply because they are not sound investments. The rents which must be charged to cover construction costs will necessarily be much higher than those in comparable existing units. Thus a new rental property has difficulty obtaining financing, regardless of the effects of rent control.

*Residential Construction in the United
States and New England*

Although the impact of rent control on residential construction can be considered using several indicators, the effects of other variables on all these indicators is much stronger than those of rent control. The primary factor influencing new residential construction and major alteration is the interest rate at which loans may be obtained. In addition, in New England, the cold temperature during the winter restricts most types of construction. Thus the impact of rent control upon new dwelling construction cannot be determined statistically, since the data do not permit separation of the effect of rent control from other factors.

Figure 1-2 displays the prime interest rate and indices of the value of new construction and major alteration of residential dwelling units throughout the United States and in New England alone. The solid line shows the national trend; the dashed line shows the New England trend. These lines are measured on the right-hand side of the graph. The dotted line indicates the prime interest rate averaged over each quarter, derived from records of the First National Bank of Boston. The prime interest rate is the rate of interest which the bank charges its favored customers for loan money. The prime rate is measured on the left-hand side of the chart, on a descending scale.

The following conclusions are demonstrated in Figure 1-2.

1. Prior to 1971, the New England index fluctuated more than the U.S. index. When the value of new residential construction and alteration rose nationwide in relation to its 1967 level, the New England value of new residential construction and alteration rose even higher. Similarly, New England experienced more pronounced declines in the value of construction contracts prior to 1971. These two indices are not seasonally adjusted, i.e., we can clearly see the effect of colder temperatures during the first quarter of each year (winter)—an effect which is more severe in Massachusetts than in the majority of the United States.

2. From 1971 to mid-1974, the New England index has consistently been lower than the national index. Nonresidential construction is considerably below the national average as well (the 1974 monthly average index is 117.2 for New England and 173.2 for the United States). We can eliminate rent control as the primary cause of the lower index, since Chapter 842 was in effect in only five communities in New England between 1971 and 1974. Most likely, residential construction in New England has dropped more than the nationwide average because construction costs have become prohibitive. However, there has been an increase in demand in other regions of the U.S. (South and West).

The indices were at the same level again during mid-1974 and during the early fourth quarter. This situation probably indicates that economic factors which lowered the New England index since 1971 are now affecting the national indicator as well.

3. The prime rate is the most important influence on construction indices. Using the left-hand scale for measurement, we can see that the prime rate changed from 6.5 percent to 8.5 percent between 1968 and early 1970; a similar decline occurred in both construction indices (note that the New England index fell as low as 45 or 50 on the right-hand scale).

The prime rate steadily decreased and settled close to 5 percent during 1971 and 1972. The construction indices rose steadily and peaked during 1972 and 1973. The lag between changes in the prime interest rate and changes in the construction indices is explained by the length of time required to arrange financing of a construction project. This lag is usually from six months to one year, as demonstrated by the graphs in Figure 1-2.

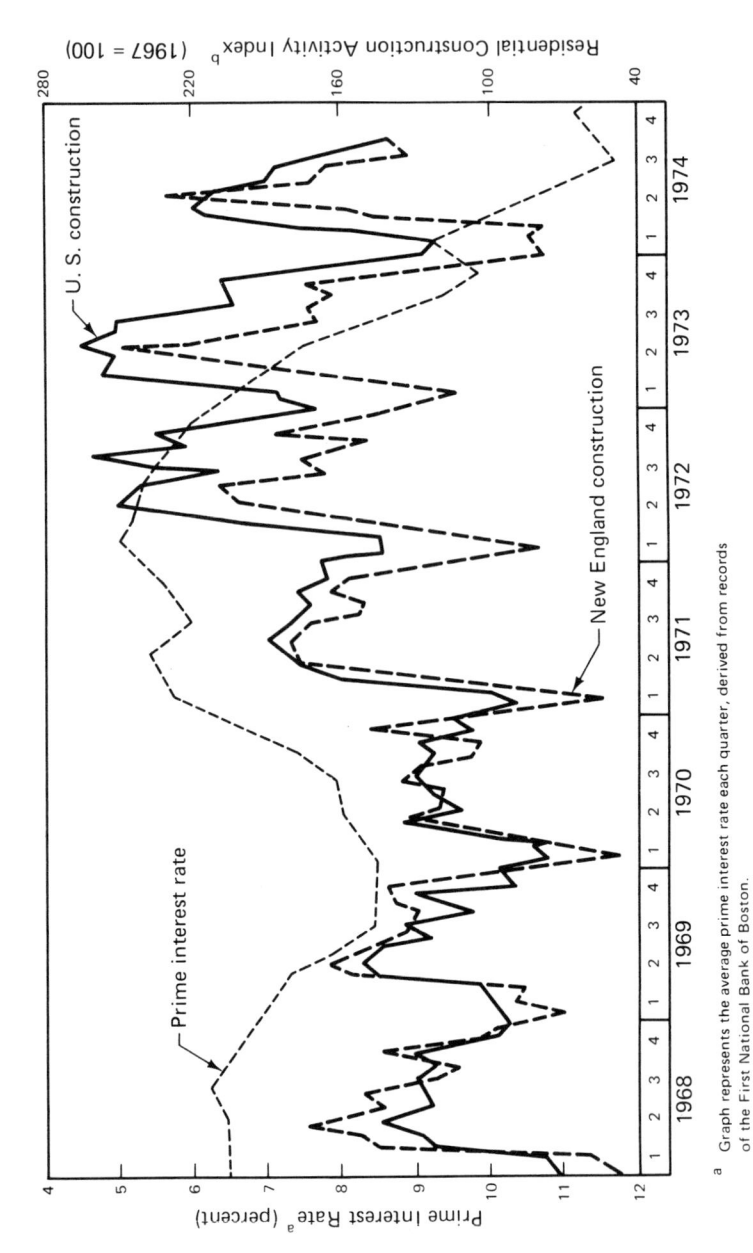

Figure 1-2. Prime Interest Rate, U.S. Residential Construction, and New England Residential Construction, 1968 to 1974.

a Graph represents the average prime interest rate each quarter, derived from records of the First National Bank of Boston.

b Graph was obtained from *New England Economic Indicators*, Federal Reserve Bank of Boston, November 1974. Index shows value of new residential construction in relation to 1967 levels, in 1967 dollars, not seasonally adjusted.

Construction and Financial Indicators

As illustrated by Table 1-19(a)-(c), construction activity is proportionately lower in Massachusetts than throughout the United States. Savings on deposit, a primary source of mortgage money, is also proportionately lower in Massachusetts than throughout the United States. Real estate loans, reflecting the patterns described above, are slightly lower in Massachusetts than throughout the United States. New England savings on deposit and real estate loans, however, are above the national average; thus Massachusetts is faring much worse than its neighboring states with respect to the savings and real estate loan indicators.

Table 1-19(a)
Construction Activity: Value of Construction Contracts for Residential Buildings (Not Seasonally Adjusted)

1974 Monthly Average	Percent Increase Over 1967 Levels
United States	+82%
New England	+49%
Massachusetts	+47%

Source: New England Economic Indicators, October 1974, Published by the Federal Reserve Bank of Boston, Data based on Dodge Reports.

Table 1-19(b)
Financial Indicators (Seasonally Adjusted)–Savings on Deposit

1974 Monthly Average	Percent Increase Over 1967 Levels
United States	+68%
New England	+70%
Massachusetts	+56%

Table 1-19(c)
Real Estate Loans (Seasonally Adjusted)

1974 Monthly Average	Percent Increase Over 1967 Levels
United States	+52%
New England	+65%
Massachusetts	+51%

Building Permit Activity in Rent-Controlled
Versus Noncontrolled Communities

Proponents of rent control often state that rent control causes landlords to increase maintenance and repair and does not prevent new construction (since new units are exempt from controls). Opponents of rent control, however, claim that rent control leads to a deterioration of rental housing and stifles new dwelling construction (because of fear that new units would, sometime in the future, be placed under control).

One indicator of levels of new construction is the number of dwelling units in structures for which building permits were obtained. An estimated 95 percent of structures receiving permits are actually constructed. In most communities, records are kept that summarize new residential construction by type of dwelling (allowing us to separate permits for multifamily units). Most building departments, however, do not summarize the estimated dollar value of new multiunit construction.

Thus we attempted to compile an accurate set of figures which would describe, in detail, the number of permits issued by each community for different types of construction. We originally sought statistics about construction work actually completed, but these data are not recorded by local building departments (which are the primary sources for the state agencies we contacted).

An examination of the level of construction of multifamily units is difficult if each year is considered separately. The total fluctuates widely from one year to another. Thus, in an attempt to isolate the impact of rent control, we grouped the years 1968-1970 and 1971-1973 together; the percentage change in permits issued for multifamily units was then easily derived for "before" and "during" rent control.

The total number of multifamily units for which permits were issued increased in 16 out of the 22 communities between the years 1968-1970 and 1971-1973. All five rent-controlled communities experienced increases; the average increase for controlled communities, moreover, exceeded the average increase for the 17 noncontrolled cities and towns. (See Table 1-20.)

Residential Construction in Boston Before
and During Rent Control

Statistics obtained from the Boston Redevelopment Authority (BRA) give a detailed breakdown of new construction in Boston. Table 1-21 describes new dwelling units by type of financing and year of completion.

The data supports the following conclusions:

1. Between 1968 and 1970, construction of privately owned dwelling units declined by more than 46 percent (1,706 units in 1968, 915 units in 1970). In

Table 1-20
Permits Issued for Multifamily Units: 1968-73[a]

City/Town	Number of Multifamily Units for Which Permit Was Issued 1968-1970	1971-1973	Percentage Change
Boston	3,863	4,534	+17.4%
Brookline	416	1,012	+140.4
Cambridge	1,766	2,662	+50.7
Lynn	263	1,485	+464.6
Somerville	313	483	+54.3
Five Rent-Controlled	6,626	10,176	+53.6
Seventeen Noncontrolled	18,584	25,783	+38.7

[a]The figures include new residential construction, both public and private.

1971, only 653 units were constructed; none were built in 1972; and 402 private units were built in 1973. (The data do not substantiate developers' claims that rent control has hampered private construction in Boston. Prior to the adoption of Chapter 842, Boston already faced plummetting rates of new private residential construction.)

2. Between 1968 and 1973, an average of 187 low-income public housing units were constructed annually. In 1973, 863 units were built. By April 24, 1974, 33 more units had already been constructed, and 510 additional units were under construction.

Chapter 842 was not officially adopted in Boston until January 1973. The effect on new construction, therefore, would not be apparent until after that date. However, the lag time between planning and completion of construction must also be considered. Table 1-21 demonstrates the number of units *completed*. The decrease in new construction as displayed in Table 1-21, therefore, cannot be associated with Chapter 842.

New Multifamily Construction in Rent-Controlled Communities

Urban Planning Aid has developed a breakdown of new multifamily construction from 1968 to 1973 in rent-controlled communities, which is shown in Table 1-22. Subsidized and unsubsidized units authorized by building permits are displayed separately. The data support the following conclusions:

1. Subsidized multifamily units [public housing, FHA 221 (d) 3, and 236] authorized by building permits increased from 3,892 between 1968 and 1970 to 5,711 between 1971 and 1973—an increase of 47 percent.

Table 1-21
Number of Dwelling Units by Completion Year and by Financing in Boston

Year	Public Housing	Subsidized Moderate Income	All Subsidized	Private FHA-Insured	Non-Subsidized Private	Total Private	Total Private and Subsidized
1968	186	274	460	—	1,706	1,706	2,166
1969	288	497	785	444	545	989	1,774
1970	208	1,365	1,573	—	915	915	2,488
Total 1968-1970	682	2,136	2,818	444	3,166	3,610	6,428
1971	—	917	917	624	29	653	1,570
1972	252	734	986	—	—	—	986
1973	863	1,560	2,423	—	402	402	2,825
Total 1971-1973	1,115	3,211	4,326	624	431	1,055	5,381
1974 Through April 24	333	3	336	—	—	—	336
Under Construction	510	2,057	2,567	710	529	1,239	3,806
Total 1968-April 24, 1974	2,130	5,350	7,480	1,068	3,597	9,330	12,145

Table 1-22
Dwelling Units Authorized by Building Permits Structures with Three or More Units (From Local Records)

City/Town	1968 S	1968 US	1969 S	1969 US	1970 S	1970 US	1968-1970 S	1968-1970 US
Boston	1,201	1,156	715	371	394	26	2,310	1,553
Brookline	0	35	100	0	71	207	171	242
Cambridge	573	95	0	51	634	90	1,207	236
Somerville	0	44	0	101	110	58	110	203
Lynn	94	24	0	103	0	42	94	169
Total	1,868	1,354	815	626	1,209	423	3,892	2,403
								6,295

City/Town	1971 S	1971 US	1972 S	1972 US	1973 S	1973 US	1971-1973 S	1971-1973 US
Boston	985	81	1,583	1,014	732	139	3,300	1,234
Brookline	0	58	130	793	0	31	130	882
Cambridge	427	190	747	332	354	392	1,528	914
Somerville	0	173	0	144	80	86	80	403
Lynn	346	126	0	48	327	443	673	617
Total	1,758	628	2,460	2,331	1,493	1,091	5,711	4,050
								9,761

S = Public Housing, FHA 221 (d) 3 and 236.
US = Unsubsidized, including FHA insured housing.
Source: Urban Planning Aid.

2. Simultaneously, *un*subsidized multifamily units authorized by building permits rose from 2,403 between 1968 and 1970 to 4,050 between 1971 and 1973—an increase of 69 percent.

3. The percentage changes (between 1968 and 1970 and 1971 through 1973) in the number of subsidized multifamily units issued permits were increases in Boston (43 percent), Cambridge (27 percent), and Lynn (616 percent) and decreases in Brookline (24 percent) and Somerville (27 percent).

4. The percentage changes between 1968 and 1970 and 1971 through 1973 in the number of private multifamily dwelling units issued permits were increases in Brookline (264 percent), Cambridge (287 percent), Somerville (99 percent), and Lynn (265 percent) and a decrease only in Boston (21 percent).

5. Based upon U.P.A.'s calculations, adoption of Chapter 842 has not prevented construction of new multifamily dwelling units. Furthermore, construction of private dwelling structures increased more rapidly in all controlled communities except Boston.

6. Prior to the adoption of Chapter 842, in the five communities, 38 out of every 100 new multifamily units were not subsidized. During the years 1971-1973, 41 out of every 100 new multifamily units were not subsidized. Clearly, new private multifamily construction increased during rent control, both in absolute numbers and in relation to unsubsidized construction.

Eviction Control as Protection for Tenants

The procedures set up by rent and eviction controls prevent landlords from enacting "arbitrary rent increases and evictions."[9] The rent control board acts as a screening device, requiring the landlord to obtain a certificate of eviction before going to the district court level. The rent control board will grant a certificate only if the landlord can prove that an eviction is justifiable.

Table 1-23 displays some summary process (eviction) writs entered in selected district courts. The table demonstrates that the "annual volume of eviction cases in rent-controlled municipalities declined substantially—e.g., by 38 percent in Boston over the past three years,[b] while evictions in noncontrolled cities were

Table 1-23
Summary Process (Eviction) Writs Entered in Selected District Courts

Rent-Controlled Cities	1967	1968	1969	1970	1971	1972	1973
Boston							
Dorchester[c]	1,881	2,998	2,048	1,994	1,679	1,569	1,269
Roxbury[c]	2,349	2,256	2,393	3,080	2,469	1,319	1,311
Brighton[c]	402	552	648	645	493	285	336
W. Roxbury	447	538	695	705	643	658	447
E. Boston	142	234	266	134	376	312	195
S. Boston	690	657	577	473	497	384	196
Charlestown	154	175	146	114	226	140	188
Municipal Court[c]	406	485	581	566	453	284	300
Housing Court[c]	–	–	–	–	–	–	742[a]
Subtotal	6,471	7,895	7,354	7,711	6,483	4,951	4,789
Brookline	101	131	195	209	144	103	88
Cambridge[d]	241	308	352	401	394	495	347
Somerville	241	188	310	390	365	382	233
Lynn[e]	350	343	520	493	514	408	213[b]
Total	7,404	8,845	8,731	9,204	7,900	6,339	5,670

[b]Comparing 1969 and 1973 figures.

	Year Ending June 30						
Noncontrolled Municipalities (Selected)	1967	1968	1969	1970	1971	1972	1973
Brockton	241	233	237	315	334	382	454
Chelsea	224	229	245	207	205	224	230
Chicopee	20	53	52	58	67	63	74
Fall River	201	215	280	202	217	233	245
Fitchburg	33	44	73	56	68	78	229
Framingham	144	103	128	147	163	148	215
Holyoke	44	57	61	99	76	65	82
Lawrence	165	160	251	266	297	348	326
Lowell	357	567	593	577	553	498	633
Malden (Medford, Everett)	266	335	378	442	418	388	389
Marlboro	40	52	50	65	59	85	56
New Bedford	264	312	348	462	400	397	400
Northampton	51	39	41	60	69	54	104
Quincy (Weymouth)	194	241	273	253	243	272	399
Pittsfield	80	88	100	95	107	130	126
Springfield	357	439	518	579	635	633	655
Taunton	53	66	95	96	99	102	98
Waltham (Watertown)	104	122	178	157	131	139	137
Worcester (Central)	413	551	538	611	625	619	712
Total[f]	4,561	5,672	6,043	6,526	7,114	7,022	8,033
Grand Total	11,965	14,517	14,774	15,730	15,014	13,361	13,703

[a]Includes about 75 transfer cases already included in district court statistics.

[b]Indicates start of eviction controls.

[c]Serves area with high concentration of rent-controlled units.

[d]Third E. Middlesex District Court also covering Arlington and Belmont.

[e]Southern Essex District Court, also covering Marblehead, Nahant, Saugus, Swampscott.

[f]For all Massachusetts District Courts in noncontrolled municipalities, including those not listed.

Note: Data reflects all writs entered in the district court, which may cover surrounding communities as well.

Source: Urban Planning Aid, March 16, 1974, from the Annual Report to the Justices of the Supreme Judicial Court by the Executive Secretary, including statistics of the district courts, as updated and supplemented by data from the Boston Municipal Court and the Boston Housing Court.

increasing."[10] Eviction cases declined by 55 percent in Brookline, 25 percent in Somerville, and 59 percent in Lynn (which only began to use eviction controls in 1973). Cambridge eviction cases declined 1 percent in comparison with its 1969 levels, but decreased nearly 30 percent between 1972 and 1973.

During the same interval (1969 to 1973), Brockton's eviction caseload increased 91 percent; Quincy and Weymouth, 46 percent; Worcester Central, 32 percent; and Springfield, 26 percent. The average rise in eviction cases for noncontrolled municipalities was 33 percent; for rent-controlled communities, cases decreased by an average of 35 percent.

Clearly, the number of eviction writs decreased in rent-controlled communities because of the "initial screening" provided by the board's review. The data demonstrate that eviction controls serve their intended purpose by preventing unjustifiable eviction attempts.

Time Period for Decisions from the Rent Control Board

Table 1-24 displays the average time span between the filing of the petition and the decision. The different time spans reflect the varying levels of detail required by each administrative agency.

Table 1-24
Administrative Functions—Time Span[a]

Boston	*Brookline*
Petition Filed	Petition Filed
Data Processing: 2 Days	Request to Landlord to Appear for Audit: 2 Weeks
Notice to Tenants: 2 Days	
Tenants' Responses: 15 Days	Audit Completed: 4 Weeks
Hearing and Inspection: 15 Days (if Necessary)	Hearing: 3 Weeks
	Decision: 3 Weeks
Decision: 5-10 Days	
Total: 4-6 Weeks	Total: 12 Weeks
Cambridge	*Somerville*
Petition Filed	Petition Filed
Hearing: 2-3 Weeks	Notify Tenants: 1 Day
Decision: 4-5 Weeks	Hearing: 3 Weeks
	Decision: 1-2 Weeks
Total: 6-8 Weeks	Total: 4-5 Weeks

[a]Approximate length of time between filing of petition and decision by the rent control board (November 1974). The length of time varies in each individual case due to factors beyond the control of the administrative staff (landlord delays, holidays, postponed meetings, etc.).

2 Local Administration of Chapter 842

Introduction

The purpose of this chapter is to assess the local administrative experience with rent control under Chapter 842, the present version of which is reprinted in Appendix A.

Toward this end, field research has been conducted in five communities, which at one time or another have accepted the act (Boston, Brookline, Cambridge, Lynn, and Somerville) and in one community, which has been operating a rent grievance program (Waltham). Four of the municipalities, Boston, Brookline, Cambridge, and Somerville, were researched in depth because they currently administer rent control under Chapter 842. The results of this research are contained in four case studies which appear at the end of this chapter. Lynn was not analyzed in depth, because that city recently revoked its acceptance of Chapter 842. The administrative experience that it had with the act was abortive and uninstructive—except to demonstrate that appointment of a highly biased board (in this case tenant-biased) can only lead to disaster. Waltham was dropped from the study because the tenant-initiated grievance system in that city differs so markedly from the prior approval approach to rent regulation of Chapter 842 that it offers few if any administrative lessons. We simply note, in passing, that the Waltham Rent Review Board has had problems obtaining sufficient financial support from the city; it has also had difficulties in securing the full cooperation of the local building department on inspections. In addition, the board's workload—averaging about 30 cases a year—suggests a low level of utilization by tenants, which was also characteristic of Boston's rent grievance experience.

Conclusions

The following conclusions emerge from the case studies of the four rent-controlled communities:

1. In the absence of state level administrative guidelines, and as a result of the flexibility in Chapter 842, the Massachusetts communities that have adopted rent control have varied enormously in their methods of implementing the statute. The four communities we studied have each followed their own individual approaches to registration, rollback, hearings, adjustments, evictions,

and compliance enforcement, as well as organization structure established to administer these functions.

2. A comparative analysis of the four rent-controlled communities reveals that, in the absence of a centralized source of data collection and information on rent control administrative practice, there has perforce been a duplication of effort across the four communities in many of the programs' development aspects, management functions, and activities carried on by local boards and administrators.

3. The comparative analysis of the four rent-controlled communities also reveals that, despite some serious problems in the beginning which affected all of them, the calibre of local rent-control administration has been improving steadily with each year's experience under Chapter 842. We find no current evidence of either widescale administrative abuses of the statute by local boards and administrators or of excessively large backlogs of unprocessed cases, as some have claimed. In fact, we have been greatly impressed by the professionalism and conscientiousness of the board members, executive directors, and administrators interviewed during the course of the field research. We have been equally impressed with the degree of systematization developed by each community regarding the processing of adjustments and evictions.

4. A comparison of Boston with the other three communities indicates that its degree of prior experience with rent control is a major factor in the board's or administration's ability to prepare adequately for the implementation of Chapter 842. The rapidly increasing proficiency of the other communities in administering the statute also bears testimony to this factor. It is therefore impossible to understate the importance of instituting a state-level source of information and assistance—especially for additional communities that might be contemplating the acceptance of Chapter 842.

5. Even in the four experienced rent-controlled communities, data collection and statistical analysis appear to receive secondary priority. This is due in part to the pressure of everyday work, which draws staff energy away from long-term research needs, and in part to the cost of ambitious research and statistics programs in relation to the number of controlled units (in all but the case of Boston). These factors, combined with the fact that most of the nonrent-controlled communities probably have a narrower base of professional expertise than do the ones that have already adopted the act, underscore the need for a state-level, centralized source of research and statistics to support local rent control administration. The cost of a centrally organized research function may well be less than the sum of the present local expenditures on this same activity.

6. If the board approach is selected and the statutory requirement for board involvement in all rent adjustment hearings is maintained, key prerequisites for the board's effective operation are:

a. A large reservoir of resident professional and business people who are sufficiently motivated and civic spirited to give abundant amounts of their time and conscientious efforts on a voluntary unpaid basis.

b. A significant degree of real estate knowledge and experience represented in the background and/or training of at least some board members.
c. Careful screening of potential board members—preferably by the chairman and executive director—with recommendations by them to the appointing authority.
d. Board members who are not radical advocates of some ideological point of view or one-sided proponents of landlord or tenant interests.
e. Significant levels of open and honest communication and cooperation between board and staff members, supported by mutual understanding and trust, agreement on respective roles and responsibilities, and substantial clear delegations of authority from the board to the staff.

7. Additional factors which contribute importantly to the effective functioning of both rent control boards and administrations appear to be the following:

a. Adequate levels of financial support for rent-control administration from the general fund of the local community.
b. Conscientious recruitment of competent staff who are paid professional level salaries and delegated significant amounts of responsibility.
c. Close working relations between the rent control board or administrator and other municipal agencies, and effective public relations between the rent control board or administrator and the community at large.
d. A comprehensive array of administrative machinery in place (board/administrator, staff, rules and regulations, procedures and forms) and statistical research substantially completed (base year, interim cost increases, and so on) *before* the imposition of a rent rollback, and/or an initial general adjustment.

8. The administrator approach appears to offer the virtue of speed in processing the workload, but it contains the potential drawbacks of (1) bias in one-man decision-making and (2) focusing local political opposition to rent control on one individual. The board approach provides the advantages of (1) balanced decision-making (if the board members are selected wisely), and (2) diffusing local political opposition to rent control by offering an umbrella under which operating staff can take shelter. The board approach has the potential disadvantages of (1) requiring more time for caseload processing (due in part to interactions and possible disagreements between board and staff) and (2) having to secure a number of qualified, unpaid volunteers to put in large amounts of time.

9. For rent control to gain acceptance in a community, landlords must know and be confident that they can obtain rent increases for increases in their operating expenses with a minimum of delay, and tenants must know and be confident that the board or administrator will enforce Chapter 842 fully and evenhandedly and, in particular, that rent increases will be limited to the amount required to cover landlords' legitimate cost increases.

10. Local administration of rent control must be flexible enough to make

reasonable exceptions that will prevent gross inequities and extreme hardships, such as, for example, (1) by requiring that steep but otherwise allowable rent increases be phased and (2) by swiftly granting rent adjustments that adequately cover increased operating expenses.

The material in the balance of this chapter was used to recommend changes in Chapter 842 to the State Legislature's Committee on Local Affairs. These recommendations were designed to modify the statute in a way that would facilitate local administration of rent control. They were based on the experiences of local rent control officials with Chapter 842. The detailed rationale for the statutory changes which we proposed comes from the case studies which appear later in this chapter.

Experience with Chapter 842—Brookline

Declaration of Emergency

The executive director observed that what started out as an emergency measure may now have become an essential long-term requirement for avoiding nationalization of the rental housing industry.

Chapter 842, by its very nature, is geared to urbanized metropolitan communities that are, or may be in the future, suffering shortages of rental housing. For this reason, argue Brookline rent-control officials, it is unlikely that Chapter 842 would ever be adopted by communities with less than 50,000 population. Most of these smaller communities are metropolitan and have comparatively high vacancy rates. (Amherst may be an exception.) Nevertheless, they should at least have the option of adopting Chapter 842 in the event that a housing shortage of emergency proportions may at some future date affect them.

Acceptance and Revocation

No comments were elicited that have a direct bearing on this section of the statute.

Definitions

The same Brookline town meeting which adopted Chapter 842 also adopted Article 30 of the town by-laws, which places rental units in Brookline's owner-occupied two- and three-family houses under rent control. Although they are explicitly exempt under Chapter 842, the Town was able to place these units under control by using their own special enabling statute (Chapter 843). The Brookline Rent Control Board subsequently initiated registration of all owner-occupied two's and three's along with the controlled units. In April of 1971, however, registration of owner-occupied two's and three's was discontinued after the town meeting amended Article 30 of the by-laws by deleting control of these units.

The second Marshall House case indicates, among other things, that underlying the intent of Chapter 842—in exempting from control rental units in owner-occupied two-family or three-family houses—is the assumption that owners of such houses typically are not professional real estate operators and, by living on the scene, can provide better services to their tenants than are received by tenants in other types of units.

Brookline rent-control officials argue that Chapter 842, by exempting all units constructed or converted from nonhousing to a housing use on or after January 1, 1969, has as its explicit intent the avoidance of discouraging new rental housing construction. Nevertheless, they are strongly aware of contentions by bankers and builders that the mere *existence* of rent control puts a psychological damper on new construction in the controlled community. They point out, however, that nationwide—especially in urban industrialized states and more especially in the Northeast—new residential construction has been declining for a variety of factors, only one of which may be rent control (for example, increased labor and material costs, inflated capital costs, diminishing availability of buildable land, and so on). They conclude, however, that if Chapter 842 is to be extended beyond December 31, 1975, movement of the cutoff date for exempting new construction forward beyond January 1, 1969 would not only give credence to the "psychological damper" argument, but might also make that argument *true*.

In applying the "new construction" exemption to units that are gutted by fire and subsequently rebuilt, the question arises as to whether such buildings come under the heading of new construction and are thus exempt from rent control, or under the nonexempt categories of rehabilitation or remodeling. The Brookline Rent Control Board, in interpreting the intent of the statute, has exempted from controls buildings for which they judge the amount of rehabilitation to be so great as to be tantamount to new construction. (These exemptions are granted only on a case-by-case basis rather than under a general regulation such as the one promulgated by the Boston Rent Control Administrator.) The rationale for exempting such units is that situations in which comparatively large amounts of capital are expended to restore otherwise uninhabitable rental housing to the community are equivalent to new construction situations. The board does not, however, regard subdivisions of rental properties, for example, conversion of an existing structure from six apartments to twelve apartments by adding interior walls, to be new construction.

The board does believe that Chapter 842 leaves too much discretion to local communities in determining what constitutes new construction for exempt purposes. If the legislature feels the new construction exemption should apply to total or partial rehabilitation, remodeling, or renovation, or to some of these, the statute should explicitly and clearly specify which of these categories are exempt. If, on the other hand, the legislature wishes to leave some discretion to local communities on this point, the statute should have added to the section on new construction exemption words such as "... and units which in the opinion of the rent control board constitute new construction."

Brookline rent-control officials believe a modified Chapter 842 should not exempt from control FHA and MHFA rental units constructed before January 1, 1969 (or, presumably, rental units *converted* from private to FHA or MHFA units before January 1, 1969). They also point out that many tenant groups would take issue with the proposed 1969 cutoff for FHA units, citing serious management and maintenance problems with FHA units built since that time.

Chapter 842 exempts from control rental units in hotels, motels, inns, tourist homes, and rooming or boarding houses which are rented primarily to transient guests *for a period of less than 14 consecutive days.* A problem arises in connection with the application of this part of the statute when some of the rooms are rented for less than 14 days and others more. The Brookline Rent Control Board grants the exemption only if *more than half* of the rooms meet the less-than-14-day requirement, although it is not clear whether that is the intent of the law. This approach can become an administrative nightmare, because the percentage of rooms renting for less than 14 days can fluctuate significantly even in the same rooming house, for example, from one week to another. Under the circumstances, administration of this part of Chapter 842 would be enormously simplified if the statute omitted the less-than-14-day requirement and either exempted or controlled *all* hotels, motels, inns, tourist homes, and rooming or boarding houses.

State Assistance and Review

Because Brookline adopted rent control on September 29, 1970, the town's six-month rent rollback date was March of 1970. However, as indicated above, implementation of the actual rollback was held up for four months—until February of 1971. The confusion attendant upon the administrative startup of a program of the scope and complexity of rent and eviction control was severely aggravated in Brookline by this litigation-caused delay. Landlords began to file petitions for rent adjustments almost immediately, that is, in October of 1970. But the rent control board could not begin acting on these petitions until February of 1971 because of the court-imposed injunction.

Hiring staff, acquiring budgetary funding, making suggestions to the board regarding forms and procedures, getting the board and staff to trust each other and accept each other's points of view, writing regulations, and establishing standards for case-by-case decision making were major activities that had to be initiated and completed during the early months of rent control in Brookline. These activities had to be undertaken in an atmosphere of controversy and confusion, with tenants and landlords telephoning virtually continuously or, in some cases, lining up in the outer hall of the building with requests for information or complaints. As a result, the startup period of rent control in Brookline was very difficult, and it was virtually impossible for the board and staff to carry out registrations and process landlord and tenant petitions swiftly and smoothly.

As indicated above, startup problems of any community which adopts Chapter 842 are enormous.[a] The adopting community desperately needs guidance and technical assistance in dealing with these problems. The executive director of the Brookline Rent Control Board receives numerous telephone calls from other communities contemplating the adoption of Chapter 842. Their needs appear to be (1) for guidance in avoiding the problems and pitfalls experienced by other communities in launching rent control, and (2) assistance with the development of implementing regulations, systems, forms, and procedures. Presently, he provides help to communities that request it on a voluntary after-hours basis. It seems clear, from the Brookline executive director's experience, that the lack of availability of technical assistance from the Massachusetts Department of Community Affairs (DCA) has discouraged several communities which might have otherwise adopted Chapter 842.

The Brookline Rent Control Board has been attempting to collect reliable statistics on the impact of rent control on property maintenance and property values, landlord's incomes and profits, and tax abatements. Sources of information have included primarily the rent control files and the tax assessor's records. The research effort has been conducted under the direction of one of the board members, who is, of course, part-time and unpaid. It has proved time consuming and difficult to establish a valid data base, and the research has necessarily had to take a lower order of priority than the board's primary mission of rent and eviction regulation. Based on their experience in this important but underattended area, Brookline rent-control officials conclude that the Massachusetts Department of Community Affairs—as presently mandated under Chapter 842—can and should play the major role in conducting research and collecting statistics on the local impact of rent control for local administrative use in support of the setting of local policy and decision-making criteria.

Chapter 842 mandated the establishment of a Bureau of Rental Housing within the Department of Community Affairs to assist and monitor local implementation of rent control. The executive branch never funded this bureau, arguing that not enough communities had adopted rent control to make the expenditure worthwhile. Brookline rent-control officials contend that a substantially greater number of communities might have adopted Chapter 842 if they

---
[a]Unless, of course, that community has had prior experience with rent control, under its own special enabling legislation, for example.

could have turned to a DCA Bureau of Rental Housing for technical assistance and startup support.

Local Rent Board or Administrator

Administratively, Chapter 842 establishes two alternatives at the local level: a rent board or an administrator. The appropriate choice depends on a variety of factors. Brookline's experience in comparison with that of Boston suggests that sheer size of the controlled housing stock should be a key determinant of which alternative is selected. A city the size of Boston apparently cannot process work rapidly enough under the board approach, regardless of whether there are 15 board members or three board members. On the other hand, for the most part it appears that a town of the size of Brookline *can* manage its workload under the board approach, as long as investigatory and hearing functions are delegated to staff people effectively and in a manner consistent with the statute. Carrying the Brookline-Boston comparison further, it appears that the administrator approach has processing speed as its primary advantage, because the administrator is answerable in the final analysis only to the Mayor, City Manager, or Board of Selectmen, while the executive director of the board is answerable to all of the board members. A serious disadvantage of the administrator approach is that it seems to focus political reactions to rent-control policies and decisions onto one person, whose effectiveness can, as a result, easily be undermined. Under the board system, accountability is somewhat more diffuse.

Chapter 842 provides that rent control boards and administrators be appointed by Mayors, City Managers, and Selectmen. Tenant groups have from time to time advocated election of boards and administrators by the public, instead. Brookline rent-control officials argue that the preponderance of tenants in the electorate would virtually guarantee a lopsided board, and it would probably be too strongly biased toward tenant interests. They stress the importance of balance and moderation on the board for rational decision making that will gain acceptance in both the landlord and tenant communities. They also emphasize the need for providing guidance to local chief executives to ensure that their appointments are judicious ones.

Another argument they offer against public election of board members is that this process would probably limit opportunities for board membership to those who have the time and money to campaign—criteria which are not likely to guarantee selection of qualified and effective board members. Gubernatorial appointment of local boards, another alternative that has been suggested, would not necessarily depoliticize the process.

The Brookline experience also suggests that, given the extraordinary amount of time board members must put in, it might be advisable to pay them for their time as well as their expenses. However, since most municipal boards and commissions have traditionally been based on the principal of voluntarism, this approach probably would not be likely to win local acceptance. In addition, the amount of money that would have to be expended to recompense Brookline board members fully—or to any significant degree—for the amount of time they put in, could easily raise the cost of local rent-control administration beyond the level that the town is willing to budget. In addition, substantial board salaries might attract candidates motivated by other than civic spiritual concerns.

Under Chapter 842, the board or administrator can delegate authority for the performance of any of its statutory functions to staff members in whatever manner it deems desirable (as long as one board member hears every rent adjustment case). The Brookline experience suggests that explicit, firm delegations by the board to its executive director, and from him, in turn, to the operating staff leads to a more effective regulatory program that makes maximum use of board availability and staff skills.

Maximum Rent

The board obtained initial information on which properties to register from the Brookline Tax Assessor's office. In February of 1971, Forms 1 and 2 were mailed with an explanatory cover letter to all owners of controlled properties. Landlords were required to send completed copies of Form 2 to their tenants for verification as well as to the board. Tenants proved to be very vigilant during this early period at flagging incorrect information on registration forms and bringing it to the board's attention. The board, on its part, assumed that the registration information received from landlords was accurate unless tenants of the units in question raised issues with regard to its validity. When questions did arise, the board conducted an investigation, and landlords were required to provide documentary substantiation of the data they had supplied (cancelled checks, for example).

The board continues to apply this tenant verification system to the information received from landlords (1) because it seems to have worked well and (2) because any other more systematic monitoring approach would be prohibitively expensive.

All the registration information the board receives on a property is transferred to punch cards and magnetic tape. In addition, the completed forms on property are stored in a file folder. Thereafter, the information is updated and/or changed only when a rent adjustment is granted for the property using Forms DPD1 and DPD2, as appropriate. All registration information on controlled properties, including the completed forms and any other parts of the property file folder, is open to the general public. Tenant and landlord attorneys frequently visit the board offices to review file folders in preparation for cases. Brookline landlords have expressed a desire to have the folders maintained as private information, but the board has not taken this approach.

Prosecution is, of course, the sanction for willful nonregistration. When the initial notices requiring registration were sent out in February, a deadline of March 30, 1971 was set for the return of the forms. This deadline was extended for individual landlords if they could show "good cause." Most landlords did in fact register prior to the end of March. By the time the present executive director joined the board, in March of 1972, compliance with registration requirements was virtually 100 percent. He estimates now that the board experiences no more than one or two nonregistration complaints and trials per year, and most of these involve landlord claims that their property is exempt.

The Brookline experience suggests that comprehensive registration is a vital ingredient of effective rent regulation, because the information obtained in registration forms comprises the core of the data base, which the rent control board uses for policy setting and decision making.

In Brookline, the six-month rent rollback meant, effectively, a two and a half year rollback for landlords who had two-year leases with their tenants which expired within the six months prior to the town's adoption of Chapter 842. As a result, many landlords were economically hurt by the rollback, and an instant backlog of petitions and, in many cases, angry petitioners was created. The number of landlords adversely affected through the lease process would have been substantially reduced if the rollback period had been three months instead. It is debatable, however, whether a three-month rollback is sufficient to "normalize" all rents arbitrarily raised by landlords in anticipation of rent control.

Another problem with the rollback provision in Brookline has been its application to properties that move from an exempt status to a controlled status long after the community adopted Chapter 842 (for example, when the owner-occupant of a two- or three-family house sells the house to someone who will not live in it). If the property comes under rent control two or three years after local adoption of Chapter 842, the question arises as to what level rents should be rolled back.

Maximum Rent Adjustment

The history of general adjustments in maximum rents granted by the Brookline Rent Control Board begins early in the period after adoption of Chapter 842. The first general adjustment granted by the board, in July of 1971, was the largest ever granted. It came primarily as a response to a workload that was getting out of control. Rent adjustment petitions were piling up unacted upon, landlords were complaining bitterly, and the board was severely understaffed and overworked in the Spring of 1971. As a result, they were simply unable to hear enough petitions rapidly enough to gain control of the growing backlog. Accordingly, the board initiated efforts to determine rental housing landlords' cost increases between January 1, 1968 and January 1, 1971, in support of the granting of a general rent adjustment that would reflect these cost increases. The board's hope was that most landlords who had individual petitions pending, unacted upon by the board, would withdraw them after the general adjustment was granted. The general adjustment that was ultimately granted in 1971 by the board was based on a complicated mathematical formula applied to data derived from the Institute of Real Estate Management's Apartment Building Income and Expense Analysis.

After this first general adjustment was granted, some landlords withdrew their individual petitions. As time went on, increasing numbers of landlords accepted the general adjustment and withdrew their petitions. The rent-control staff encouraged this process by counseling landlords with petitions that were pending. They assisted landlords in reviewing their expenses, determining their net return, and assessing the likelihood of success or failure of their petitions, and the possibility of a rent reduction based on a board hearing. Additional general adjustments were granted by the board in 1972 and 1973, supplemented by the same counseling process. In this way the board first stabilized, then reduced, and ultimately eliminated the backlog of individual rent-adjustment petitions that had built up in the first hectic year of operation.

The board passed a second general adjustment in June 1972, effective as of September 1972. This adjustment involved a dollar-for-dollar pass through of the actual increase in the 1972 tax rate.

A third general adjustment of 3 percent was voted by the board in June 1973, effective as of September 1973, based on two factors: (1) a 1.8 percent increase in all costs associated with rental housing between the first quarters of 1972 and 1973, and (2) a 1.2 percent projected increase in the 1973 tax rate (which turned out to be accurate). Landlords who had received individual adjustments between October 1972 and June 1973 were only allowed to qualify for the tax portion of the increase, because fuel cost increases had already been accounted for in their individual adjustments.

In June 1974, for the first time, the board voted not to grant a general adjustment. Individual petitions have increased since that time. As a result, the board voted in October to discontinue before-the-fact advisory opinions on capital improvements indefinitely in order to concentrate on individual rent adjustment petitions and prevent the buildup of a backlog in that vital area.

Brookline rent-control officials and board members would like guidance on the definition and application of fair net return formulas, but they feel this guidance should come administratively through a DCA Bureau of Rental Housing, rather than statutorily through Chapter 842. Their belief is that flexibility is essential because different formulas may work well for different communities. DCA's role should be to assure that whatever formulas are being used are fair and administered equitably.

The Brookline experience suggests that Chapter 842 should explicitly grant local rent control boards an option with regard to general adjustments (for taxes, fuel costs, etc.)—namely, of basing them either on a uniform percentage increase or on a tailored dollar-for-dollar pass through prorated across the individual units in each controlled property.

In Brookline, as elsewhere, landlords have faced a serious time lag in passing through tax increases to tenants via general adjustments. The general adjustments have been based on complicated and time-consuming computations. It took time to collect the data required for these computations. And the general adjustment for taxes, even though voted by the board on June 1 in 1972 and 1973, was not made effective until September 1 each time. The net result has been that landlords have not been getting back their tax increases through generally adjusted rent increases from January through August of the tax years and have only begun to realize relief through the general adjustment in the month of September. To alleviate this problem, Brookline presently allows landlords to include their tax increases with other operating expense increases in their individual rent-adjustment petitions.

The Brookline Rent Control Board promulgated a regulation, which has since been rescinded, enabling them to order rent *reductions* without hearings until the code violations in a controlled property were remedied. The purpose of this regulation was to stimulate more aggressive enforcement of local codes by the town's health department. The board felt that their control of rents provided natural economic leverage that could be used to force better code compliance among owners of controlled properties. The board's code regulation threatened landlords with a 10 percent rent reduction for minor violations (noncertified, not dangerous to health or safety, etc.) and a 20 percent reduction for major violations. Inspections by the health department which turned up code violations in controlled properties were to be transmitted to the board for action. Inspections by the board's staff (in response to tenant complaints, for example) which turned up suspected violations were to be referred to the health department inspectors for verification. The board was to enforce rent reductions in units out of code compliance until they received written notice from the health department that the property had been brought up to code.

Implementation of this regulation became an administrative nightmare. The health department failed to let the board know, in many cases, whether and when violations had been corrected, landlords complained when their original rents were not promptly reinstated, in many cases the health department gave landlords extra time to do repair work, the board itself was deluged with calls requesting extensions, and reinstatement dates began to mount. Finally, the board was taken to court by landlords challenging the rent-reduction regulation. The court decision did not invalidate or even question the intent of the regulation, but it did order the board to conduct a hearing prior to deciding on a rent reduction for code violations.

The board finally rescinded their rent-reduction regulation, having decided that they could accomplish the same objective through board-initiated hearings and hearings on tenants petitions. During the entire period that the regulation was in force, the board ordered no more than about 20 rent reductions for code violations.

In connection with the processing of rent-adjustment petitions, it is important to point out that, in conformance with Chapter 842, the Brookline Rent Control Board goes well beyond the simple adjudication of rent increase requests. The board's staff investigators not only fully audit landlords' expenses but also thoroughly inspect their properties in every case of a rent-increase petition. Major code violations, and in many cases, suspected violations, are referred to the local health department. Expense audits and property inspections are also carried out in response to complaints of tenants in controlled properties. In connection with serious code violations that are identified in these inspections (and verified by the local health department), the rent control board frequently issues "conditional decisions" regarding standards of maintenance. These decisions either make allowed rent increases conditional upon the landlord's correction of certain violations or deficiencies within 60 days, or they levy rent reductions if certain conditions are not remedied by the landlord within 60 days. By using economic leverage in a carrot-stick way, Brookline rent-control officials believe their approach to implementation of Chapter 842 not only cushions tenants of controlled properties from inordinate rent increases but also provides them with better living conditions and contributes to *improved* maintenance of the controlled stock.

Rent Adjustment Hearings

In practice, paired staffing of rent-adjustment cases fosters a highly productive and cooperative working relationship between the board and the staff. Because the staff investigator performs most of the data gathering, he is more likely to have detailed facts and knowledge of the case at his fingertips than is the board member assigned to the case. The board member, on the other hand, has a broad policy overview by virtue of his sitting on final determinations of all cases. Generally, the board member and staff investigator working on a case agree on a recommendation. When they do not, the staff investigator is encouraged to offer a counter recommendation, and both proposed decisions are considered by the board. This arrangement provides a framework within which staff members feel free to make serious inputs to board decisions, and it enforces their sense of professionalism and responsibility. (Not infrequently, the board will support the recommendation of the staff investigator over that of the board member assigned to a case.)

The Brookline approach to rent adjustment hearings is markedly different from that practiced by Cambridge. In Cambridge, board members do not sit on individual cases. Instead, "prehearings" are conducted by hearing examiners, all of whom are attorneys. Cambridge complies with the Chapter 842 requirement that at least one board member hear a rent adjustment case by conducting pro forma hearings of cases within the context of their weekly meetings.

A comparison of the variation between the Brookline and Cambridge approaches suggests that a modified Chapter 842 should, among other things, specify whether in fact a rent control board can delegate authority to staff to conduct rent-adjustment hearings. The advantage of this delegation, of course, would be its impact on local boards' abilities to speed up processing of their caseloads with heavier use of paid staff in the hearing process. A potential danger is "rubber stamp" review by the boards-of-staff recommendations—in the absence of board participation in the hearing process, with possible abdication by the board of its all-important policy development and policy compliance roles.

Evictions

Brookline rent-control officials believe that condominium conversion is not just grounds for eviction under grounds (10) in Section 9 of Chapter 842. Conversions themselves cannot, of course, be prevented under present laws. The Brookline Rent Control Board will only grant applications for certificates of eviction for purposes of condominium conversion to bona fide purchasors of the condominium units if they have fully executed deeds. Evictions of this kind are granted under grounds (8) of Section 10. They argue that permitting wholesale eviction of tenants from rent-controlled properties for condominium conversion would further aggravate the shortage of low- and moderate-income rental housing in Brookline, and this is counter of the aims and intent of Chapter 842.

Judicial Review

Under Section 10 of Chapter 842, the district courts have exclusive original jurisdiction over all petition for review of local rent control board decisions and actions. The Brookline experience suggests that mandating initiation of the review process at the district-court level may be inefficient, since aggrieved parties who are dissatisfied with district court decisions can and usually do press on to superior court anyway. Brookline's Chapter 843 gives the aggrieved party the choice of going either to district court or superior court by providing both courts with concurrent jurisdiction over the review of local board determinations. Brookline rent-control officials argue that Chapter 842 should be altered to adopt this approach because it would speed up the entire review process.

Civil Remedies

Table 2-1 shows a statistical summary of civil litigation in which the Brookline Rent Control Board was involved during calendar year 1973. As can be seen, the preponderant element in the civil litigation workload was rent adjustment appeals by landlords in the Brookline Municipal Court, which represented almost half the cases. The same pattern held true during calendar year 1972. Rent adjustment appeals by landlords in superior court and eviction appeals in appeals court were the other major types of cases during the year 1973, with due process litigation accounting for somewhat more of the work in 1972. There

Table 2-1
Summary of Civil Litigation in Brookline

	Number Active	Number Disposed of	Number Pending
Brookline Municipal Court			
Rent adjustment appeals (by LL)	50(39)	21(11)	29(28)
Rent adjustment appeals (by T)	3 (3)	1 (1)	2 (2)
Eviction appeals	10 (7)	7 (6)	3 (1)
Exemption appeals	2 (3)	0 (1)	2 (2)
Miscellaneous appeals	3 (0)	2 (0)	1 (0)
Applications to enforce summons	6 (1)	5 (1)	0 (0)
Applications for contempt citation	1 (0)	1 (0)	0 (0)
Interventions in civil action	2 (2)	0 (0)	2 (2)
Due process	0 (7)	0 (7)	0 (0)
Superior Court			
Rent adjustment appeals (by LL)	14 (2)	5 (0)	9 (2)
Eviction appeals	2 (2)	0 (1)	2 (1)
Exemption appeals	3 (3)	1 (0)	2 (2)
Miscellaneous appeals	1 (0)	1 (0)	0 (0)
Mandamus	0 (1)	0 (1)	0 (0)
Equity bills seeking injunctive relief	7 (7)	2 (4)	5 (6)
Appeals Court			
Rent adjustment appeals (by LL)	1 (0)	0 (0)	1 (0)
Supreme Judicial Court			
Mandamus	1 (0)	1 (0)	0 (0)
Federal District Court			
Civil rights actions	1 (0)	1 (0)	0 (0)

was a backlog of 58 active pending civil cases existing at the end of calendar year 1973, and up to 50 percent of them were from the 1972 year-end backlog. About 30 percent of the backlog was in superior court, with virtually all of the balance in Brookline Municipal Court. In all, the board was involved in 106 civil cases during calendar year 1973 and 77 civil cases during calendar year 1972.

Chapter 842 (Section 11, Part b1) gives the rent control board the right to bring an action or seek a settlement in the event that a tenant victimized by overcharges fails to do so within 30 days of the violation. The executive director of the Brookline Rent Control Board feels that this provision of the statute is probably superfluous because, in practice, his board and other local boards leave it solely to the aggrieved tenant to bring such actions.

An additional change in Chapter 842, which would speed up the process of judicial review and probably diminish the number of reversals by the superior court of Brookline Rent Control Board decisions, would be the treatment of board action as actions of any state agency, as provided for under the Administrative Procedures Act. This would limit superior court review of local rent control board decisions to administrative review (that is, on the record) rather than the present *de novo* review.

Criminal Penalties

During the early months after adoption of Chapter 842 in Brookline, enforcement activities resulted in a larger number of criminal prosecutions by the board's legal staff. Most of these criminal actions were brought against property owners either for failure to register with the board or for habitual charges or receipt of overpayments. More recently, however, the volume of criminal prosecution activity has dropped to a marginal level. The board still receives daily correspondence and telephone calls from tenants complaining of overcharges, but these are not dealt with via board-initiated criminal action. The board seeks to, and is almost always successful at persuading tenants to deduct the amount of the overpayment(s) from their future rent. This alternative is preferred by most tenants because it avoids the necessity of going through the criminal complaint process, which would involve taking time off from work or school, for example, to testify at a court hearing. The board reserves prosecutorial action only for those cases in which the landlord has been warned repeatedly and continues to overcharge "habitually."

In most cases, the board is reluctant to prosecute for two reasons. First, they have been "left at the altar" frequently in the past by aggrieved tenants who failed to show up in court after they had arrived at an outside financial settlement. Second, in criminal cases landlords can appeal decisions to, and ask for a *de novo* trial in superior court. The board's legal staff cannot continue the prosecution there because jurisdiction reverts to the Middlesex County District

Attorney.b He apparently does not give rent control a high priority, and delegates prosecutorial responsibility to one of his assistants. And, more often than not, the municipal court's decision is overturned. In any event, once the case reaches superior court, the district attorney's office handles all negotiations with the landlord's attorney if the latter decides that he wishes to gain an out-of-court settlement. This situation destroys the continuity of local enforcement and diminishes some of the credibility of the local rent control board. In the opinion of the executive director, it is the primary weak spot in the enforcement powers conferred on local boards by Chapter 842.

In those rare instances when a tenant insists on prosecuting a landlord, he is advised by the board to lodge a complaint with the Brookline Municipal Court. The board's legal department will represent him if he follows through.

Nothing in the Brookline Rent Control Board's experience suggests any reason to alter the criminal penalties associated with Chapter 842.

Currently, compliance with registration requirements appears to be under control in Brookline. The publicity given to early convictions of landlords for nonregistration appears to have all but eliminated deliberate avoidance of registration. In cases where there is a question whether property is exempt, or where the property's status may be changing from controlled to exempt, the landlord remains subject to the board's registration requirements and hearing procedures until the exempt status is officially decided. For example, if an individual were to purchase a two-family house and seek to occupy one of the units and rent the other, he must obtain a certificate of exemption from the rent control board, if the former owner did not occupy the house.

Table 2-2 presents a quantitative summary of the criminal prosecution activity engaged in by the Brookline Rent Control Board in calendar year 1973. Most of the activity (39 cases) involved complaints related to excessive rent charges—processed in Brookline Municipal Court. A small number of nonregistration complaints (four) were also sought. Thirty-two criminal cases were resolved by the board's staff investigators.

Termination

An important question raised by the Legislature's extension of Chapter 842 from April 1, 1975 to December 31, 1975 is whether cities and towns must convene Council (Town) meetings to *readopt* Chapter 842 after April 1, 1975.

Severability

No comments were offered on this section of the Act.

---

bTechnically, the District Attorney's office handles all criminal prosecutions in superior court. The district attorney's office does allow the board to prosecute.

Table 2-2
Summary of Criminal Prosecution Activity in Brookline

	Excessive Rent	*Non-registration*	*False Information*
Brookline Municipal Court			
Complaints sought	39	4	0
Complaints denied	9	0	0
Complaints resolved	8	4	0
Complaints issued	22	0	0
Complaints tried	6	0	0
Complaints pending	16	0	0
Superior Court			
Appeals tried de novo	2	0	0
Office Investigation			
Investigation letters	20	0	0
Cases resolved	32	4	0

Note: Comparable statistics for the 1972 calendar year were not available.

Experience with Chapter 842—Somerville

Declaration of Emergency

No pertinent comments or observations.

Acceptance and Revocation

No comments or observations having a direct bearing on this section of Chapter 842.

Definitions

Section 3(b)(7) of Chapter 842 provides the option of exempting units from control (up to 25 percent of the total rental units in the community) for which rent charges exceed locally specified limits. Except for a small number of units built during the last five years, and therefore exempt under Section 3(b)(2), Somerville has virtually no "luxury" housing. Accordingly, the Somerville Rent Control Board has taken no action under the optional luxury housing exemption of Chapter 842.

Exemption of condominiums under Section 3(b)(4) of Chapter 842 and the corollary issue of eviction control in the case of condominium conversions have not arisen in Somerville because there are no condominiums, and there have been no conversions in the city. In fact, there are very few older large apartment buildings in the city.

There is only one large FHA rental property in Somerville. The HUD Regional Office General Counsel sent the rent control board's general counsel a letter stating that FHA housing is not subject to local rent control. The board exempted the property, not because it was FHA subsidized but rather because it was not occupied until after January 1, 1969. Some of the landlords in Somerville have been leasing their properties to the local housing authority solely because it enables them to obtain higher rents than the board would allow for their units.

Somerville has experienced problems with college-owned properties in relation to Section 3(b)(5) of Chapter 842. Tufts and M.I.T. sought to have private homes which they leased to faculty members and students exempted from rent control as "rental units in any ... college ... dormitory operated exclusively for charitable or educational purposes ..." The Somerville Rent Control Board opposed this exemption on the grounds that these homes were not dormitories in the strict sense. The district court upheld the colleges, however, and the exemptions were granted.

The Somerville Rent Control Board has a specific regulation pertaining to rehabilitated housing, which specifies that a "substantially" rehabilitated property will be regarded as new construction and exempted under Section 3(b)(2) of Chapter 842 only if the landlord invests more than half of the property's present value in rehabilitation, renovation, or repair.

The Somerville Rent Control Board defines new construction not as units *built* after January 1, 1969, but, rather, as units for which a certificate of occupancy was issued after that date. The latter indicator signifies that the building was not virtually complete and available for occupancy until after January 1, 1969. As proof that the new construction exemption has succeeded in not choking off additions to or upkeep of the rental housing supply in Somerville, the Mayor cites the building permit statistics listed in Table 2-3.

State Assistance and Review

The executive director and general counsel of the Somerville Rent Control Board point out that DCA assistance and review would have been very helpful at the startup of their program. A central information gathering and disseminating agency could have been helpful by (1) identifying for them just what problems other communities had had with implementation of Chapter 842 and how they addressed those problems, (2) providing guidance and assistance to them with

Table 2-3
Building Permit Statistics in Somerville

Number of Permits Issued	Calendar Year
490	1968
425	1969
586	1970
492	1971
683	1972
681	1973
700+ (projected)	1974

the ongoing problems of a mature program, (3) setting forth model regulations they could have used as a reference point for establishing their own, and conducting educational seminars they could have attended on problems of rent control administration, (4) convening periodic meetings of local rent-control staffs which they could have attended for sharing the state of the art, and (5) collecting and disseminating statistical information which they could use, demonstrating the impact of rent control on the local rental housing market, abatements, upkeep, taxes, etc.

Local Board or Administrator

The executive director and general counsel of the Somerville Rent Control Board prefer the board form to the administrator approach because they feel it provides a broader base of input to the decision-making process.

Maximum Rent

If Chapter 842 is extended beyond December 31, 1975, the executive director and general counsel of the Somerville Rent Control Board would like to have Section 6(b) amended to explicitly exempt all rent control registration records from Chapter 66, Section 10(b) (the disclosure statute) and Chapter 4 (which defines public records).

Maximum Rent Adjustment

The board had, at one time, a regulation under which they could order rent reductions for substandard controlled properties until the owners brought them up to code. The board had only a handful of cases under this regulation, however.

Rent Adjustment Hearings

The experience of the Somerville Rent Control Board with general adjustments indicates that Section 8(b) of Chapter 842 should be amended so that it explicitly allows local rent control boards to promulgate general adjustments on a dollar-for-dollar basis as well as a percentage basis.

Evictions

In eviction cases, the Somerville District Court has on occasion ordered the establishment of an interest bearing escrow account at a bank for rent payments, pending settlement of the case. The executive director and general counsel of the Somerville Rent Control Board favor the use of interest bearing escrow accounts held by neutral third parties to avoid situations in which tenants live rent-free in apartments while undergoing protracted eviction proceedings. Another variation is to have the court designate the landlord's and tenant's attorneys as joint escrow agents. In the case of eviction proceedings, rent money would be paid into the account by the tenant; in overcharge cases the landlord would pay the money in. Provisions for banks or attorneys to act as escrow agents in disputed rent-control cases could be set forth in a revised Section 9 of Chapter 842, in regulations promulgated by a DCA Bureau of Rental Housing pursuant to their monitoring and review of local implementation of Chapter 842, or, perhaps preferably, under revised state laws dealing with administration of the court system.

Judicial Review

Some local rent-control administrators have suggested that a revised Chapter 842 should make Section 14 of Chapter 30-A (the Administrative Procedures Act), which limits judicial review of state agency decisions to an on-the-record as opposed to a *de novo* review, fully applicable to judicial review of local rent control board decisions. The general counsel to the Somerville Rent Control Board opposes this change because, in his view, due process requirements would then necessitate that local rent control boards give tenants and landlords full adversary proceedings. The Somerville Rent Control Board is not equipped for this approach. In addition, he argues that the courts are better prepared than rent control boards for engaging in factfinding types of hearings, with formal rules of evidence and all the rest. He further contends that state agencies are exempt from *de novo* judicial review in Chapter 30-A because it was felt that, in most cases, a state agency has an established body of rules, regulations, procedures, and policy precedents and that, for this reason, on-the-record reviews of their decisions were feasible and preferable. On the other hand, the general counsel feels that the framers of Chapter 842 probably assumed that newly formed rent control boards would typically lack established rules and regulations, and that administrative review of their determinations by the courts would therefore be neither practical nor reliable.

Three frequently cited advantages of limiting judicial review of local rent control cases to on-the-record review are (1) a shortening of the time it takes to process appeals, (2) a reduction of the frequency with which courts overturn local rulings, and (3) a diminution of the courts opportunities to effectively set rent-control policies without regard for local policies. The general counsel to the Somerville Rent Control Board argues that on-the-record review can be as time-consuming as *de novo* review, and courts can still end up setting rent-control policies by rejecting local regulations and/or objecting to the way they were applied by the local board. In addition, he points out that court reversals have primarily affected the Boston Administrator and the Brookline Board and, to a much lesser extent, the Cambridge Board and the Somerville Board.[c]

Civil Remedies

Private attorneys acting for tenants have been successful in obtaining triple damage judgments against landlords in cases where the court finds that the landlord willfully violated the rent-control statute. These judgments can at times amount to severe (and even crippling) financial penalties. The Somerville Rent Control Board cooperates with private attorneys by making their records available in such cases. The board itself has never brought an action for triple damages.

Criminal Penalties

The board had a few prosecutions the first year it was in operation, but almost none since then. They usually encourage tenants to recoup the amount of the overcharge through subsequent rent payments, and most tenants take this route. If tenants decide to prosecute landlords, they must retain their own attorneys; the board's general counsel does not represent them. Often, however, the board ends up in court as a party to suits between landlords and tenants.

[c]The Town of Brookline has a case pending before the supreme judicial court contesting whether Chapter 842 does in fact have as its intent *de novo* judicial review of rent-control cases. The Third District Court recently ruled that Chapter 842 does have as its intent *de novo* judicial review.

The board has found that when they are successful in obtaining a district court judgment that would impose a fine or a jail sentence on a landlord, he invariably appeals the case to superior court, where the decision is overturned. With regard to enforcement of Chapter 842, there appear to be two problems at this judicial level. First, all criminal complaints at the superior-court level must be brought in the name of the commonwealth, which thereby confers prosecutorial responsibility on the district attorney's office. Unfortunately, the district attorney's office in Middlesex County (as elsewhere) knows very little about rent control. A second problem is the apparent attitude of superior court judges, who seem to feel that loss of rent overcharges and perhaps also the general adjustment to which he would otherwise be entitled are severe enough penalties for any landlord who violates the statute. In addition, superior court judges do not seem to view violation of Chapter 842 as important enough to occupy criminal court time.

The board's general counsel does take a landlord into criminal court if repeated attempts to get the landlord to register his property have failed. However, he has never had to go past the complaint stage with the court clerk in such cases. When the court clerk affirms that the property in question is in fact subject to rent control and must be registered with the board, the landlord almost invariably complies. In those rare cases when a landlord persists in not registering his property, he first receives a series of increasingly threatening letters. If he does not register after three months of this correspondence, the general counsel visits him in person and generally takes every possible step to avoid court action.

Termination

The Mayor of Somerville claims that his city has the lowest apartment vacancy rate of any greater Boston community. Accordingly, he advocates extension of Chapter 842 beyond December 31, 1975, from Somerville's point of view.

Experience with Chapter 842—Cambridge

The principal problem with eviction control under Chapter 842 in Cambridge has been the excessive length of time required for processing and granting certificates. Table 1-14 shows the median times required for applications for certificates of eviction to pass through various stages of processing for each of the past two years. As of the first part of this year, it was still taking a median time of 8 to 9 weeks to get decisions made on evictions, whether for nonpayment of rent or on other grounds. While this represents a substantial improvement over the early part of 1973, it is, of course, far from satisfactory. The executive director believes he can shorten the overall process to an average of 18 days.

Declaration of Emergency

No specific comments on this section.

Acceptance and Revocation

No observations bearing directly on this section.

Definitions

The executive director of the Cambridge Rent Control Board supports the concept of the 25 percent optional luxury housing exemption, provided "luxury" is defined on the basis of rents exceeding a certain amount. In practice, however, Cambridge has had trouble implementing a luxury housing exemption, primarily because the board has not registered all the rental units. As a consequence, granting of a luxury housing exemption could lead to a situation in which the board unknowingly exempted more than 25 percent of the total rental units in the municipality. Moreover, rents are required on every residential building for the computation of rent limits above which the luxury housing category begins.

The board grants new construction exemptions to all units "substantially reconstructed" without stipulating a dollar expenditure requirement the way that Boston does. The variability of the way this issue is treated by individual boards indicates, according to the Cambridge board's executive director, that Chapter 842 should be amended either to explicitly exclude or explicitly include major rehabilitation under the exempt category for new construction. Apparently, this exemption alternative motivates some landlords to let their buildings run down so that they can evict the tenants, rehabilitate the property, get it exempted from rent control, and raise the rents. The net result of major rehabilitation in such cases is to create a higher rental property which is no longer available to low-income families and no longer subject to rent control.

In addition, the executive director believes that Chapter 842 should be amended to define explicitly the meaning of construction completed on or after January 1, 1969. He suggests that the least ambiguous definition may be "first occupied on or after January 1, 1969."

Experience in Cambridge also suggests that "rented primarily to transient guests for a period of less than fourteen consecutive days" is not a useful benchmark for exempting rental units in hotels, motels, inns, tourist homes, and rooming or boarding houses. Apparently, this terminology comes from old federal rent-control statutes and was designed to exempt seasonal rentals. Today there are rooming houses devoted partly to transient rentals and partly to continuous (year-round) rentals. The question arises as to whether "rental primarily to transient guests" means more than 50 percent of the guests must be transient, more than half of the units must be rented to transients, or something else. Another important reason for framing Section 2(b)(1) more explicitly is to prevent or make it more difficult for landlords to get their apartment houses decontrolled simply by asserting that they are now rooming houses. The executive director suggests that perhaps the least ambiguous and most workable exemption criterion for this purpose is the concept of an established tenancy. Under this formulation, if the landlord is legally required to go to court to evict the occupant of a unit in a so-called hotel, motel, inn, tourist home, or rooming or boarding house, then a tenancy has been established that should be subject to control under Chapter 842. If, on the other hand, the landlord can evict the occupant without court process, no tenancy has been established and the unit is exempt. This formulation could be applied on a percentage basis to the units in hotels, motels, etc., to determine whether they are exempt from control. If no legal tenancies are found to have been established in more than half of the units, then the whole building would be declared exempt from control.

State Assistance and Review

The executive director has written several times to the governor requesting that he establish a bureau of rental housing within DCA, as mandated by Chapter 842. An important reason for DCA monitoring and assistance of local rent control is that local boards and administrators cannot stand back and objectively evaluate and redirect their own performance. The needs of Cambridge and other local rent control boards suggest, according to the executive director, that an initial bureau of rental housing, staffing, plan, and budget might be set up as shown in Table 2-4.

The bureau should have as the primary elements of its mission (1) centralization of data collection and analysis in support of research on fair base rents and the local impact of Chapter 842, (2) dissemination of the state of the rent control art to local boards and administrators, and (3) monitoring of local implementation of Chapter 842 to assure conformance with the statute, consistency of interpretation, and equity of application.

Local Rent Board or Administrator

Rent control in Cambridge began with an administrator. Controversial decisions by the administrator caused enormous legal problems and engendered community-wide hostility toward rent control. As a result, the city council finally concluded that the administrator approach was an unmitigated failure and voted

Table 2-4
Proposed Budget and Staffing for DCA Bureau of Rental Housing

Staff	Salaries	Totals
Director (1)	$22-25,000	$22-25,000
Assistant Director (1)	14-16,000	14-16,000
Statistical Expert (1)	16-18,000	16-18,000
Computer Programmer (1)	16-18,000	16-18,000
Field Representatives (4)	12-14,000	48-56,000
Clerks (3)	8,000	24,000
Estimated Annual Payroll		$140-157,000
Miscellaneous Expenses[a]		40,000
		$180-197,000

[a]Computertime, office equipment, local travel, etc.

to change over to a board approach. In the opinion of the executive director, under a board the Cambridge rent control program has been converted from a failure to an emergent success. He opposes the concept of a paid board, feeling that the present unpaid approach is more appropriate to the board's role and functions.

Maximum Rent

Section 6(a) of Chapter 842 requires that rents of controlled units be rolled back to levels six months prior to the date of acceptance of the act by the municipality, and Section 2 implies that this rollback must take effect 30 days after the municipality's acceptance of the act. The executive director of the Cambridge Rent Control Board feels that this 30-day/6-month rollback provision of Chapter 842 is responsible for the major administrative problems of rent control. The rollback provision requires an "infant" rent-control agency to perform an "adult" task rapidly and without error. Effective implementation of the rollback provision requires a full board, functioning staff, registration forms, hearing procedures, and a comprehensive set of regulations.

The experience of Cambridge as well as other communities that have adopted Chapter 842 shows conclusively that these administrative prerequisites simply cannot be put into place successfully within 30 days after the act's acceptance. The executive director points out that somewhat smoother startups in those cities with pre-842 rent-control experience (Boston and Cambridge) attests to the level of experience and expertise required to deal with mandatory rent rollbacks and the instant backlog of petitions they create.

Moreover, by mandating a six-month rent rollback, Chapter 842 assumes that rents charged six months prior to the local adoption of Chapter 842 were fair rents, both in an absolute and a comparative sense. If the adopting community can rebut this assumption by proving, with reliable statistical evidence, that rents charged six months prior to the acts' acceptance were in fact not fair, then, according to the executive director, the community should be able to move administratively to a fair base right away. The mandatory rollback provision in Chapter 842 prevents the community from doing so.

Accordingly, the executive director recommends that Section 6(a) of Chapter 842 be altered in one of the following ways:

1. Allow the community 90 days or more after adoption of Chapter 842 for implementing the rollback and to provide time for gearing up to handle the inevitable influx of individual rent-adjustment petitions.

2. Eliminate the rollback provision altogether and require the community—within 90 days or more after adoption of Chapter 842—to complete all pertinent studies and grant a general adjustment against a base year or month for which the study results will show that rents are fair.

The executive director prefers the second of these alternatives. If the statute were changed in this way, new local rent control boards could ease themselves into their regulatory programs on a planned and deliberate basis—without the arbitrary application of 6-month rollbacks 30 days into the program. Ideally, the gearing-up process would consist of the following sequence of steps:

1. Select board and staff
2. Set up office
3. Train board and staff
4. Draft regulations and print forms[d]
5. Inform landlords and tenants about Chapter 842
6. Register units, analyze data, and identify fair-rent base year or month
7. Conduct public hearing(s) on a general adjustment
8. Grant a general adjustment by updating rents from a fair base year or month

This process assumes that the board would, of course, begin enforcing the eviction part of Chapter 842 immediately after the act takes effect in the community and that all rent increases after the act takes effect would require hearings on individual petitions.

It is difficult, if not impossible, for local rent control boards to be certain they are controlling all the units that should be controlled when they cannot require registration of all rental units [those claiming to be exempt under Section 3(b) as well as those that are not exempt]. The executive director of the

---
[d]Particularly important is the design of registration forms that will enable the board to obtain the kind of information needed to determine a base year (or month) in which rents are fair.

Cambridge Rent Control Board feels that Section 6(b) of Chapter 842 should authorize local boards and administrators to require registration of *all* rental units—not just controlled rental units. Landlords would then be required to petition for exemption under Section 3(b), and the local board or administrator would reach a determination based on the registration information for the property in question.

Maximum Rent Adjustment

Based on the Cambridge board's experience, the executive director concludes that general adjustments are the key to efficient and equitable implementation of Chapter 842. Establishment of a firm data base and reliable analyses of that base for purposes of computing and granting realistic general adjustments enables the board to remove most controlled rental units from the problem category. Case-by-case review is then limited to a manageable number of landlords with genuine problems not resolvable via the general adjustment. Moreover, experience shows that it is prohibitively expensive to deal with cases individually as a matter of routine rather than on an exception basis. Boards which treat every case as a problem end up creating problems.

The experience of the Cambridge Rent Control Board suggests that Section 8(b) of Chapter 842 should explicitly empower the board or administrator to make general adjustments of rents "by percentage or otherwise." In practice, the most equitable and defensible general adjustments are on a dollar-for-dollar basis. For example, the Cambridge Rent Control Board has information on what every owner of controlled properties paid to the city in real estate taxes on those properties. Accordingly, when there is a substantial tax increase, the preferred method of general adjustment might be to allow each landlord to pass on to his tenants the dollar increase (or some fraction of it) in his taxes. If Chapter 842 explicitly allowed this method, the board would not then have to compute what the average percentage tax increase amounted to on each controlled property. In addition, the dollar-for-dollar pass through is 100 percent accurate, while the average percentage pass through allows too much of an increase to some landlords and not enough to others, thereby generating additional petitions in the workload.

Another change, either in Section 7 of Chapter 842 or in implementing regulations to be developed by a DCA bureau of rental housing, which would cut administrative costs for local boards and administrators, would be explicit permission to round off rent figures to the nearest dollar. This would save the added cost of keeping records to two decimal places on all rents.

The executive director feels that Section 7 of Chapter 842 should define more clearly the concept of fair net operating income. He points out that the concept of fair net operating income is derived from the post-Korean War

Federal Rent Control Act of 1953 which in turn harks back to the post-World War II Federal Rent Control Act of 1946, and that this latter act may have been taken from an even earlier federal rent-control statute. The courts have attempted to define fair net operating income. The only precedents, however, are in public utility rate setting cases, and most rent control administrators contest the validity of this parallel.

Specifically, the executive director would like a revised Chapter 842 to give sanction to several alternative formulations of FNOI, including not only those approved by the courts (percentage return on value) but also other methods, such as percentage of gross income and preservation of net income (from some base year). Communities that have accepted the act should be able to use any of these formulations and more than one if they so choose, he believes.

If a landlord defers maintenance on his property until he is forced to do it to bring the property up to code, the board does not grant him a rent increase to cover the cost of the repairs he has made. If, on the other hand, the landlord performs maintenance work on his property before code compliance problems force him to do so, then the board capitalizes the cost of the repairs he has made and grants him an appropriate rent increase.

State laws which grant municipalities the right to have health departments and housing inspectors also restrict authority for the execution of local code enforcement to these entities. Rent control boards and administrators, on the other hand, have ongoing administrative relationships with a far greater number of housing units than local health and inspections departments are equipped to handle. Accordingly, the executive director of the Cambridge Rent Control Board would like to see an amendment either in state health and housing inspection laws or in Chapter 842 which would empower local health and building inspection departments to delegate their code enforcement authority for controlled properties to local rent control boards and administrators.

Section 7(d) of Chapter 842 gives the local board or administrator the power to remove maximum rents for any class of controlled units if the need for continuing maximum rent levels no longer exists because of sufficient construction of comparable rental units or because the demand for the class of units in question has been otherwise met. Presumably, it is under this section of the statute that local boards or administrators would invoke vacancy decontrol, a frequently suggested strategy of decontrol. The executive director of the Cambridge Rent Control Board is strongly opposed to this method of lifting controls for the following reasons:

1. The opening up of individual vacancies within a class of rental units is not in itself a sign of a diminished shortage within that class. A vacancy may occur because of landlord-tenant conflict; if the landlord was at fault, there is no reason why he should reap an economic benefit for his misdoings. A vacancy may occur because a low- or moderate-income apartment has become physically unlivable, in which case the rent control board's policy objective is to motivate

the landlord to bring it up to code and re-rent it to another low- or moderate-income family. If the unit is decontrolled, he may not be motivated to fix it up except in a way that will reap much higher rents and thereby remove the unit from the low- or moderate-income market.

2. Experience with vacancy decontrol in other states shows that it allows (and may even motivate) landlords to harass low- and moderate-income tenants (and perhaps even evict them) in hopes that by getting them to vacate the unit they will be able to escape controls. Low- and moderate-income tenants, the people who most need the protections offered by the rent-control statute, are apparently the least likely types of people to avail themselves of those protections. As a result, vacancy decontrol could produce a mass migration of low- and moderate-income families out of the community that adopts it.

3. Experience with vacancy decontrol elsewhere indicates that it forces a community's stable low- and moderate-income tenants to compete for the poorest economic values in local apartments. Under rent control, a stable local tenant is better able to find and secure a sound economic value in an apartment than an outside transient tenant because he has a greater familiarity with the local housing market and hears about attractive vacancies first. Under vacancy decontrol, landlords actually tend to raise the rents of newly vacant units to levels higher than transient tenants are willing and able to pay, while local stable tenants are left to compete for less attractive economic values in rental housing.

Rent Adjustment Hearings

The executive director urges that Section 8(a) of Chapter 842 be altered to remove the requirement that rent-adjustment hearings be conducted before the administrator or at least one member of the board. He feels that this function should be delegated to paid staff because of the time it consumes and the expertise it requires.

Evictions

With regard to Section 9(a)(5) of Chapter 842, the phrase "and in such terms that are not inconsistent with or violative of any provisions of this act" is not sufficiently specific, in the Cambridge experience, to define the kinds of leases landlords may request tenants to extend or renew.

Judicial Review

Experience with the judicial review process in Cambridge suggests that a revised Section 10 of Chapter 842 should specify that the appeal route is to superior court and not to the appellate division of the district court, in the opinion of the executive director. In addition, this section of the statute should place a time limit of, say, 21 days on all court appeals of board or administrator actions, regulations, or orders. He also believes the first appeal route should be back to the local board or administrator for an administrative or on-the-record review of the case and, again, within 21 days of the board's or administrator's original decision.

Apparently, Chapter 842 presently does not mandate either administrative or *de novo* review in appeals cases but gives the courts broad powers to determine the scope and depth of their review. This reflects the fact that the framers of the statute did not know just what kinds of local rent-control agencies would be established, how formalized a body of rules, regulations, and procedures they would have, and how much of a workload would be involved for district courts in the review of local rent-control determinations. For all these reasons, the executive director favors a continued broad power for the courts in determining the scope of judicial review.

When tenants are victorious at the district-court level, landlords frequently appeal to superior court because they can afford the cost and they feel they have a better chance at this level. Superior courts typically have large caseloads with big backlogs, and so the result of an appeal at that level usually causes an extensive delay in the ultimate decision on a rent control case. The executive director of the Cambridge Rent Control Board feels that this practice is counter to the thrust of Chapter 842; a temporary statute should produce speedy decisions that are responsive to the needs of an emergency housing situation.

Escrow accounts are not always easy to implement, in the view of the executive director, because of the difficulty of drawing up comprehensive agreements that do not omit at least one contingency that could block the release of the money.

Civil Remedies

No comment or observations bearing directly on this section arose during the field visits to Cambridge.

Criminal Penalties

The experience of the Cambridge Rent Control Board suggests that the criminal penalties provided for violation of the rent control statute, under Section 12 of Chapter 842, are not being enforced in a way that would give them any deterrent impact. Judges apparently are very reluctant to give landlords criminal records for violation of the rent-control statute. What they usually do is (without a finding of guilt) to require that the landlord pay court costs and, in the case of overcharges, return the amount overcharged to the tenant. Under these circumstances, local rent control boards are reluctant to bring criminal actions because of the likely outcome. And landlords can feel fairly safe about overcharging rents because the most they can lose is the amount of the overcharge (plus, possibly, court costs).

With regard to Section 12(b), the Cambridge experience suggests that Chapter 842 should be amended to define more specifically (1) just what constitutes a finder's fee and a service charge, (2) who can lawfully collect such charges, and (3) what must occur for such charges to be lawfully collectible. The object of Section 12(b) should be to prevent a landlord from charging *any* finder's fees and/or service charges for the opportunity to lease or rent his units, but in a way that does not put legitimate rental agents out of business. The largest problem with the interpretation and application of Section 12(b) arises when the landlord and the rental agent are two different companies but one and the same person. Apparently, some landlords look upon finder's fees and service charges as convenient mechanisms for circumventing control and increasing their effective annual rental income by one-twelfth.

Termination

The executive director of the Cambridge Rent Control Board believes that a revised Chapter 842 should include a termination date—probably five years after its extension date. Automatic termination will serve to remind communities (mayors, selectmen, landlords, and tenants) that accept the act that (1) it is only a temporary emergency measure and (2) they must take positive steps to add to and enhance their housing stock by new construction, rehabilitation, and more effective code enforcement as part of a long-term solution to the rental housing problem. In addition, if the present emergency housing crisis lasts longer than expected, five-year legislative review of Chapter 842 offers the opportunity of continued improvement of the statute based on local administrative experience, as well as maintenance of the statute's appropriateness, by keeping it responsive to changing conditions in the rental housing market.

Experience with Chapter 842–Boston

Declaration of Emergency

No pertinent observations or comments were registered.

Acceptance and Revocation

No pertinent observations or comments were registered.

Definitions

Boston's experience suggests that Section 3(b)(5) of Chapter 842 should be amended to address more explicitly the issue of which college buildings should or should not be exempt from control. For example, there is nothing in the statute regarding fraternity houses. Are they or are they not to be treated as dormitories? In addition, the statute should make clear that buildings leased by a college from private landlords and occupied by students, faculty, or other members of the college community are exempt if fees for occupancy are charged "by the head" rather than by apartment unit, even when such buildings are not licensed with the community as dormitories. Perhaps these problems could be cleared up by a short statutory definition of dormitories, suggests the assistant administrator for rents, such as "residential units owned or operated by a school or college."

In practice, there appears to be a question as to whether rehabilitation can or should ever be regarded as constituting new construction. The former administrator believes that Chapter 842 should remain silent on this point, leaving it to local boards or administrators to promulgate and apply their own regulations regarding the treatment of major rehabilitation, renovation, and repair. There is considerable variation in the way the four rent control communities treat cases of substantial rehabilitation. For example, in Somerville the cost of rehabilitation must be at least half of the present value of the building to count as new construction; in Boston it must amount to $10 thousand per unit or more. The assistant administrator for evictions suggests that there should be some broad guidelines in the statute for granting the new construction exemption in cases of substantial rehabilitation, such as, for example, "the rehabilitated units must be in new condition and comply with all local codes."

With regard to the present January 1, 1969 cutoff date for new construction, the former administrator points out that there has been relatively little rental housing construction in Boston during the past several years, except for federally subsidized construction. He claims that the primary investment motivation for the latter has been the achievement of tax shelters (unaffected by rent control) and not for obtaining competitive rates of return. If the volume of privately financed new construction has dwindled to virtually nothing across the rest of the state, as well as over recent years, and the (tax-shelter) federally subsidized activity is all that is left, then it probably makes good legislative sense to update the January 1, 1969 cutoff date. The indication would then be that new private construction could only be revived by some form of federal intervention anyway.

If, on the other hand, there has been some privately financed new construction in the nonrent controlled part of the state, then the January 1, 1969 cutoff date should probably be left intact. In that case, it might be necessary to incorporate some provision in the statute authorizing communities to exercise some form of rent and eviction control over new construction after it has reached a specified age. For example, Section 3 could be amended to authorize local adoption of tenant-initiated rent grievance and review ordinances applicable to all units constructed after January 1, 1969 after they are five-years old. Alternatively, the exemption presently granted to such units under Chapter 842 could be changed from a permanent to a temporary one, say for five years.

With reference to the issue of local control of rentals in FHA units, the former administrator points out that until quite recently FHA officials were virtually "rubber stamping" rent increases proposed by owners of their units. He admits, however, that FHA has tightened up their rent-review procedures considerably in Boston. Moreover, having never before permitted adversary proceedings on proposed rent increases, FHA recently, for the first time, granted tenants the right to file complaints. These improvements, coupled with the fact that local regulations on top of FHA control of rents can be a nightmare for landlords, leads the former administrator to conclude that increased rent-control accountability within FHA may be a preferred alternative to local control. This increased accountability should be accompanied by further tightening up of FHA rent review procedures, including the adoption of provisions for formal hearings on landlord petitions for rent increases and on tenant complaints of code violations.

In the opinion of the assistant administrator for rents, if it is legal, Chapter 842 should be revised to eliminate the exemption of FHA units. He contends that FHA regulation of rentals, even with the new procedures which allow tenants to complain, is a violation of each tenant's right to due process, because FHA only calculates what is needed to cover the mortgage. No effort is made to determine what rents are equitable.

In the opinion of the former administrator, Section 3(b)(5) of Chapter 842 is not explicit about all of the various kinds of public institutions that should be exempt from rent control. For example, Section 3(b)(5) makes no specific mention of YMCA's and YWCA's. To deal with possible exemptions that are not mentioned, a revised Chapter 842 should either enumerate them fully and unambiguously in Section 3 or grant the administrator or board explicit authority to promulgate regulations as a means of defining which public institutions are exempt.

Section 3(b)(1) exempts from controls rental *units* in hotels, motels, inns, tourist homes, and rooming or boarding homes which are rented *primarily* to transient guests for a period of less than fourteen consecutive days. The underlined words indicate the ambiguity in this exemption. To deal with this ambiguity, the Boston Rent Control Administrator promulgated a regulation that exempts *buildings* in which *more than half of the units* are occupied by transient guests.

In the opinion of the former administrator, much of the phrasing in Chapter 842 should be reworded to indicate that rents are to be determined by building rather than by unit.

The exemption of owner-occupied two- and three-family units probably reflects an attempt to avoid unnecessary political opposition to rent control, considering how numerous these kinds of buildings are. In addition, however, the former administrator points out that regulation of rents in all these small building units would create a tremendous administrative burden for local boards or administrators. The compliance officer of the rent control administration reports that there has been a problem in defining owner-occupied two- and three-family houses when there is more than one owner. Many of the problem cases would be eliminated if the wording of the exemption in Section 3(b)(6) of Chapter 842 were expanded to include "... the rental unit or units in a two-family or three-family house occupied by one or more members of the owner's immediate family." A strict interpretation of Section 3(b)(6) would place a single family home under rent control if the owner rented it and did not live there. The Chairman of the Boston Rent Control Board doubts that such is the intent of Chapter 842 and would like explicit language in the statute to exempt single family rentals.

State Assistance and Review

In the opinion of the former administrator, state assistance and review of local rent control should be funded.[e] A key issue is the scope and authority of DCA in compliance review. Considering that rent control is a local option, locally voted and funded, communities might question the role of DCA in directing their boards or administrations on how to run their rent-control program. With this factor in mind, he suggests that an appropriate compliance enforcement role for DCA might be one in which they bring to the attention of a community those instances in which it is acting in a manner not consistent with Chapter 842 and, perhaps, that it be accompanied with the power to issue "cease and desist" orders. In addition, the DCA could serve as a forum for landlord complaints about local administrative practices. Also, DCA should provide technical assistance to local boards and administrators in program development and management.

In any event, the general counsel to the rent control administration notes that establishment of a DCA Bureau of Rental Housing is mandatory—not discretionary—under Chapter 842; and for that reason he feels the executive branch must appropriate funds for the bureau whether or not it feels that enough people are affected by Chapter 842 to warrant expenditures of the money. Expenditure of state funds on a DCA Bureau of Rental Housing could well save an equivalent or greater amount of local general funds, points out the assistant administrator for

---
[e]DCA requested funding of a bureau of rental housing in each of fiscal years 1971, 1972, 1973, 1974, and 1975. The 1971 request died in committee, and the subsequent requests were struck by the Secretary of Administration and Finance. DCA has a pending request for $40 thousand for fiscal year 1976 for the bureau.

rents, if the bureau were successful in introducing greater efficiencies into local programs and in centralizing the data collection and statistical analysis functions that are now performed separately by the municipalities.

Local Rent Board or Administrator

Consistent with his views regarding the desirability of limiting the scope of judicial review of rent control, the former administrator of Boston's rent control program would add words to the following effect to Section 5(e) of Chapter 842 dealing with the board's/administrator's power to issue orders and promulgate regulations: "... including without limitation the power to define terms and conditions in this act to the extent that they are ambiguous."

Section 5(b) of Chapter 842 specifies that members of rent control boards are to receive no compensation for their services, except for necessary expenses incurred in the performance of their duties. The former administrator feels that this provision is only realistic and workable with the elimination of that part of Section 8(a) of the statute which requires all rent-adjustment hearings to be conducted before at least one member of the board. Apparently, many communities do not have a large reservoir of public spirited citizens who—on a voluntary unpaid basis—will put in the amount of work required to hear every case. In addition, it is usually very difficult to find a hard-working, unpaid board chairman who is also politically acceptable to all the concerned factions. If the concept of an unpaid board is to be preserved, then, in addition to dropping the board's hearing function, Section 8(a) should specifically authorize something like the following procedure in Cambridge, where the board has unofficially delegated the hearing function to a paid executive director and, through him, to paid staff members called hearing officers. Hearing officers should be empowered to handle cases virtually from start to finish and make fully developed recommendations to the board. Section 8(a) should indicate that the unpaid board is to serve in an advisory capacity.

The rent control administration's general counsel, on the other hand, feels that the concept of an unpaid board is impractical, given the amount of work involved. He points out that Boston had a paid board under Chapter 11 and obtained much more board involvement in day-to-day operations than is the case with the current unpaid members of the board. In addition, the general counsel believes Chapter 842 should be more explicit on what local boards or administrators must do in promulgating and publicizing regulations. Should there be public hearing requirements? Advertising requirements? Postings for a specified number of days?

The Chairman of the Boston Rent Control Board similarly feels that an unpaid board is unworkable because of the amount of hours they would have to put in to be fully functional. He is also of the opinion that the granting of subpoena powers to local boards and administrators in Section 5(d) of Chapter 842 is a mistake because (1) it can be abused, and (2) if landlords fail to provide the information required by the board or administrator, they will not get their rent increase anyway.

Maximum Rent

In the opinion of the former Boston Rent Control Administrator, Section 6 of Chapter 842 should empower the board or administrator to require registration of *all* rental units in the community, not just controlled rental units, with an exemption under Section 3 to be granted only upon receipt of a petition for the exemption. He points out that this change in the statute would probably incur the resentment of property owners who were certain to be exempt from control. They would not see the justification for having to surrender confidential information on their properties to a public regulatory body under whose regulatory purview they ultimately would not fall. Accordingly, a universal registration requirement should probably be accompanied by statutory provisions for (1) board/administrator consideration of landlord petitions not to register and/or (2) exemption from the public records statute of all registration information received from owners of rental properties that are eventually granted exemptions under Section 3 of Chapter 842.

The general counsel to the rent control administration would have preferred to see the continuance of Chapter 11 in Boston for an additional two years before the acceptance of Chapter 842. This would have given the city time to develop uniform registration procedures and to ease into full registration in preparation for Chapter 842.

The administration's compliance officer indicates that there have been problems establishing the maximum initial rent for buildings not covered by Chapter 842 when it was first accepted by the city but that have since lost their exempt status. He contends that if such a unit comes under Chapter 842 today, for the first time, it makes no sense to roll back the rents in the building to the city's rollback date of June 1972. Even though the act seems to mandate a rollback to the rents charged six months prior to its acceptance, the Boston Rent Control Administration allows the owner of a property that has come under Chapter 842 *after* its acceptance to submit an immediate rent adjustment petition on the basis of which the initial maximum rent for the unit is set.

Maximum Rent Adjustment

In one instance the supreme judicial court has said that FNOI is return on value; in another case it ruled that it is return on investment. In both cases the court, in the absence of clear statutory guidance, has either been interpreting or hypothesizing about the intent of Chapter 842. Recently, the presiding Judge of the Boston Housing Court has been overturning Boston Rent Control Administration determinations of FNOI, insisting that a specified percentage of the landlord's return on investment or equity be the basis for rent-adjustment decisions. The rent control administration's general counsel feels that court interpretations of this kind are inappropriate and only occur because Chapter 842 itself is vague about FNOI. He believes that some definitive guidance is needed in the statute.

Boston's rent control Regulation 6 sets forth the administrator's approach to fair net operating income. This regulation assumes that rents in December of 1971 were sufficient to yield landlords whatever is meant by a "fair net operating income." The rationale for this assumption was that prior to the adoption of Chapter 842 the rental housing market in Boston was whatever is meant by a "free market." The thrust of Regulation 6 is to allow landlords only those rent increases that will cover their cost increases over the costs reflected in December 1971 base rents unless the landlord can demonstrate that on December 1971 his rents were not yielding a fair net operating income (in which case he would be granted a greater increase). The intent of the regulation is to preserve the landlord's December 1971 net dollars of operating profit, with the full realization that this profit figure will decline as a percentage of gross rental income over time.

The former rent control administrator, who designed this approach to FNOI, contends that it is eminently preferable from an administrative point of view to the major approaches that have been adopted by other boards (i.e., percentage of gross income and return on value). For example, the Boston Rent Control Board, established under Chapter 10, assumed that a landlord was receiving a fair net operating income from his property if this net operating income totalled 35 percent of his gross rental income after taxes and operating expenses but before financing costs and profit.[f] If the landlord's return was found to be less than 35 percent defined this way, the board would first compute the increase in his 1968 base rents required to yield a 1968 return of 35 percent and would then grant him that increase plus the added increase necessary to cover his rising operating expenses between 1968 and 1969. This approach could (and did) result in very significant increases in the rents of some tenants. If, on the other hand, a landlord who was petitioning the board for a rent increase was found to have been receiving more than a 35 percent return, his increase was denied and the board tried to pressure him into reducing his rents. Thus, because there was no built-in assumption that pre-Chapter 10 rents were free or fair market rents, this method could have produced exorbitant rent increases or altercations with landlords about excessive historical returns.

---

[f]Initially, the cutoff figure was 40 percent; it was found to be too high and was subsequently reduced to 35 percent.

The range of fair returns that were ultimately determined are shown in Table 2-5.

Alternatively, the former rent control administrator points out that most of the conceptual and administrative problems with the former Cambridge and present Brookline approaches to FNOI stem from their reliance on return on value, which raises two objectively unanswerable questions: What is value? What is a fair rate of return? It is virtually impossible to develop comparatively defensible estimates of value, based on assessments, in Boston (and the other rent controlled communities) because of the crazy-quilt pattern of variation in assessments. Moreover, the capitalization of income approach opens up a range of 4 to 7 times gross income for the better housing stock to 1½ to 3 times income for the Dorchester-Roxbury stock.

Determining a fair rate of return is even more problematic. Some property owners advocate 12 percent, but in Boston this is out of tune with reality. Approximately ⅔ of the city's rental housing property yields about a 4 percent return on value. There was a time when this was completely satisfactory; expectations may well be only a *little* higher now. The former rent control administrator stresses the fact that at least 80 percent of Boston's tenants live in buildings with fewer than six units. Such buildings typically are not owned by sophisticated real-estate investors whose primary interest is long-term capital appreciation, but, rather, by smaller landlords who are happy if the rents yield enough to pay off the mortgage, cover taxes and maintenance, and provide them with a modest annuity for life. Moreover, he contends, increasing numbers of the sophisticated investors are no longer looking to rental housing for handsome returns on their equity, but, rather, for rapid-depreciation tax shelters. This newer style of real-estate entrepreneur typically rolls over his equity in one property to additional new properties to maximize the depreciation factor.

In light of what is the likely structure of motivation among urban real-estate investors today, the former rent control administrator contends that there simply are no solid grounds for advocating an 8 or 10 percent return on value.

Table 2-5
Range of Fair Returns

Small Building; Less Than 6 Units	20-35%[a]
Older, Larger Buildings	25-40%
Buildings Constructed or Rehabilitated Since 1960	35-50%

[a]Percent of gross rental income accounted for by net operating income after taxes and operating expenses but before financing costs and profit.

This approach would be tantamount to a policy of rent maintenance rather than rent control. He contends that a cost pass-through approach to FNOI makes the most administrative sense because (1) it obviates most arguments about what was fair prior to rent control (while retaining provisions for adjustments to eliminate demonstrable inequities), and (2) it relies on objective and reliable statistics (base rents and documented cost increases).

The key question, of course, is whether the legislature can or should write a specific formula approach to FNOI into Chapter 842. The former rent control administrator feels that the answer is no, because of the great range of diversity of rental housing and the multiplicity and variety of reasons why people invest in it. The tax shelter investor might be satisfied with a zero rate of return. The investor seeking the security of a net income for life and no mortgage after 30 years might accept a constant profit dollar, or he might be satisfied with a 5 percent rate of return (or less). No one formula approach mandated by the statute can reflect or be responsive to the full range of possible situations. On the other hand, if the legislature were to mandate a rate of return on rental housing (regardless of the range of investor motivations) that is competitive with the returns that are available in other investment alternatives, then, clearly, in today's tight money market rents would skyrocket. If the statute were to mandate a significantly lower-than-competitive fixed rate of return, landlords could be severely hurt.

On the basis of these considerations, the former Boston rent control administrator concludes that Chapter 842 should explicitly authorize communities accepting the act to adopt a variety of FNOI approaches, including not only formulas based on return on value or equity but also formulas or methods that allow pass through of increased operating expenses. The statute might also authorize boards or administrators to adopt the following key elements of the cost pass through approach:

1. To keep landlord returns as close as possible to the myriad of situations that existed prior to the acceptance of Chapter 842.

2. To allow increments to base rents large enough to preserve landlords' fixed net operating incomes after taxes and before financing, adjusted for inflation.

3. To grant individual increases (or order individual decreases) based on petitions or complaints which show that the landlord's pre-842 rents were not yielding a "fair return."

4. To limit the annual rent increase tenants must pay to a specified percentage of their present rents by requiring deferment of allowed overages to the following year(s).[g]

5. To promulgate regulations which identify specific examples of gross inequities and extreme hardships affecting tenants or landlords which could be used by the board or administrator as grounds for allowing rent increases covering more or less than the landlord's documented cost increases.

---

[g]The Boston Housing Court as ruled against this approach.

The speed with which significant cost increases can be passed along by landlords to tenants through rent increases is so important to the effective and equitable administration of Chapter 842 that the former rent control administrator believes the legislature should seriously consider incorporating in Section 7(a) of the statute the requirement that local boards or administrators conduct public hearings on general adjustments for landlords' cost increases since the rollback date no later than one month after the imposition of the rollback.

Another suggestion for increasing the speed with which rent adjustment petitions are processed comes from the chairman of the rent control board, who suggests that rent increases become collectible—in an interest-bearing escrow account until the petition is adjudicated—not less than 30 days after the date of the petition.

Section 7(d) of Chapter 842 enables the board or administrator to disallow a rent increase if the unit in question does not comply with codes due to the landlord's failure to provide normal and adequate repair and maintenance. In the opinion of the general counsel to the rent control administration, this provision is probably successful in motivating owners of controlled buildings to keep up their properties.

The rent adjustment provision of Chapter 842 is a difficult one for older, ethnic landlords of Boston's neighborhoods—particularly in the North End, Charleston, and East Boston—who have never kept financial records and have traditionally charged very low rents for cold-water flats that could never have complied with local codes. These landlords cannot afford to hire an accountant, for example, to provide them with the documentation they would need to obtain a $5 rent increase; nor might they qualify without making prohibitively costly expenditures to bring their units up to code. And yet, in the opinion of the rent board chairman, these smaller unsophisticated landlords were at one time the backbone of the city's older neighborhoods.

Rent Adjustment Hearings

The Boston and Cambridge Rent Control Boards conduct hearings on all rent-adjustment petitions as a matter of routine. In Boston, a hearing is conducted only if the tenant requests one or, of course, if the administrator on his own initiative decides to hold one. This approach has resulted in hearings being conducted in only about 25 percent of the rent-adjustment cases in Boston.

The assistant administrator for rents feels that general across-the-board adjustments are by their nature inequitable and inflationary, except immediately after a community's acceptance of Chapter 842, to provide relief from the rollback. In his view, case-by-case rental determinations are the most equitable approach.

Evictions

The former administrator strongly believes that eviction on the grounds of nonpayment of rent should remain subject to control under Chapter 842 because, in his view, it is the nonpayment grounds that have been traditionally abused by landlords.

There appears to be a question as to whether the landlord's intent to rehabilitate a controlled unit constitutes just grounds for eviction from that unit under Section 9(a)(10) "for any other just cause... not in conflict with the provisions and purposes of this act." The presiding judge of the Boston Housing Court claims, citing the supreme judicial court's "Mayo" decision, that rehabilitation is not just grounds; the former Boston Rent Control Administrator disagrees. Section 9 of Chapter 842 should expressly indicate whether, in fact, an owner of a controlled unit can bring an action to recover possession of that unit for the purpose of rehabilitation. The issue is an important one. If Chapter 842 serves to discourage rehabilitation, then deterioration and abandonment could be the ultimate end products.

The Boston Rent Control Administration has an eviction regulation covering rehabilitation which requires that before a landlord can initiate eviction proceedings for rehabilitation purposes, he must demonstrate that the requisite financing has been secured, that he has formulated a concrete rehabilitation plan, that he has successfully applied for building permits, and that he has made provisions for relocating tenants to comparable housing accommodations. The assistant administrator for evictions suggests that it might be possible to leave this aspect of Section 9 to local regulations and interpretations.

Tenants groups frequently claim that conversion of apartment units to condominiums is a method being used by landlords to circumvent rent control [by obtaining exemptions under Section 3(b)(4)] and that increasing numbers of such conversions are draining the rental housing market, especially in the City of Boston. Whether condominium conversion can or should be prohibited by statute in tight rental markets is a difficult question, which goes beyond the scope of provisions of Chapter 842 to the issue of how to balance property owners' rights against the rights of individual tenants.[h] The Boston Rent Control Administration regulates evictions of tenants for condominium conversions through Section 9 of Chapter 842. In the opinion of the compliance officer, it is Section 9 of the statute that is most pertinent to the issue of condominium conversion. In Boston, a landlord, acting as the owner or agent for a bona fide buyer of one of the condominiums-to-be in his building, can apply to the rent control administration for a certificate of eviction *just for that unit*, if and only if (1) he has executed an unconditional purchase and sales agreement with the prospective buyer, and (2) the buyer's financing for the purchase has been fully

---

[h]In any event, the place for regulating condominium conversions and sales is probably not in a rent-control statute.

arranged. Notwithstanding this procedure, no tenant can be evicted from his apartment for condominium conversion prior to the time his lease expires.

The rent control administration's compliance officer would like to see the Boston approach embodied in an amended Section 9(a)(8) of Chapter 842. The advantage of requiring the purchasor to "almost" buy the apartment/condominium before the landlord can initiate eviction proceedings is that he then has the opportunity to see that the tenant is out of the apartment before he actually passes papers and executes the deed. In this way, the buyer avoids the problem of having to make mortgage payments on a house and a condominium while the sale of the house awaits the completion of eviction proceedings (which can take as long as six months). In contrast, the Brookline Rent Control Board requires a final sale with a fully executed deed to the condominium before they will entertain an application for an eviction certificate under Section 9(a)(8) and requires the purchasor to obtain the eviction certificate. The net effect of either approach is that owners of apartment buildings are prevented from evicting their tenants wholesale *without* having lined up legitimate buyers of the prospective condominium units.

Judicial Review

In the opinion of the former Boston Rent Control Administrator, the courts should be limited in their review of local rent-control determinations to administrative reviews of the kinds to which state agencies are subject under the Administrative Procedures Act.[i] Presently, Chapter 842 and rulings of the supreme judicial court indicate that courts have the power to engage in *de novo* review of local rent-control actions and orders. If their scope were limited to administrative review, then a question of whether a particular case of substantial rehabilitation constituted new construction or not, for example, would be answered solely by the board or administrator. Then the courts would only have to decide (on appeals) whether the locally prescribed procedures and regulations covering this matter had been properly followed and applied.

In the opinion of the former administrator, it is inconsistent with the intent of existing home-rule legislation to establish a local option regulatory program whose policies and administrative applications are left partially to the control of the courts. If local communities are to be held accountable by the legislature for the equity and efficiency of rent regulation under Chapter 842, then their general-purpose governmental bodies should be delegated responsibility for monitoring and controlling the actions of the rent control boards and administrators. In his view, the argument that local political pressures make this

---

[i]On this point, however, the rent control administration's compliance officer argues that local rent control boards and administrations do not meet the Chapter 30-A definition of state agencies.

approach unworkable is inconclusive. While tenants are more numerous, landlords have perhaps more effective access to local chief executives by virtue of their greater resources and political sophistication.

The general counsel to the Boston Rent Control Administration feels that Section 10(a) of Chapter 842 should speak more explicitly to the nature of the procedure for appealing decisions made by local boards or administrators and the scope of judicial review. Specifically, he believes the statute should set a time limit on appeals by aggrieved parties, perhaps within seven days, but up to 30 days from the date of decision with the consent of the court. In addition, the statute should be specific as to whether judicial review of local decisions is to be a *de novo*, step-by-step review of cases or an administrative or procedural review. The general counsel feels that *de novo* review undermines the credibility of local rent control boards and administrators. He prefers a procedure whereby judges would be limited to the review of a certified record of the case.

In the opinion of the assistant administrator for eviction, *de novo* review may be a more acute problem for the Boston Rent Control Administration than for other rent control boards because of the backlog in Boston courts. Ten district courts and the Boston Housing Court have jurisdiction over appeals in Boston. The district courts simply were unable to handle the volume of cases emanating from the city's housing inspection, building and public works departments, rent board, and rent control administration. In addition, most of the district court judges are not very conversant with housing law. For these reasons, the Boston Housing Court was established and granted exclusive jurisdiction over all housing-related cases. Designed to function as a "people's court" the housing court has very simple appeals procedures, which primarily involve the checkoff of a few blanks on a form. As a result, the housing court has a large backlog of cases. *De novo* reviews require full-scale trials with rules of evidence, and they are more time consuming than administrative reviews. Given the backlog of cases in the housing court, *de novo* review of decisions of the Boston Rent Control Administration can only serve to slow up final determinations considerably. At the outset, all parties to rent-control appeals resisted *de novo* review in the Boston Housing Court, even though it seems to be called for under Section 19(a) of Chapter 842, and the court was performing procedural reviews. More recently, the situation has reversed.

De novo reviews in the Boston Housing Court are apparently not in the best interests of tenants or small landlords who cannot afford the legal costs involved in the pursuit of a *de novo* case. Larger landlords are helped by *de novo* reviews at the first appellate level, because (1) they have the resources to pursue them, and (2) they have a better chance ultimately to gain a reversal of the original administrative decision of the local body. In its review, the supreme judicial court apparently *begins* with what the housing court judge did; it ignores the local decision.

Moreover, if landlords were to carry *de novo* review to its logical extreme, contends the assistant administrator for evictions, they could deliberately omit financial information from their rent-adjustment petitions and wait until their appeal is heard in the housing court to provide the added data. If the courts were restricted explicitly in Chapter 842 to a Chapter 30-A type of review of local decisions, landlords (and tenants) would either introduce all relevant information at the local administrative level or it would not be heard at all. A Chapter 30-A review of the record is wholly procedural, limiting the Judge to an assessment of whether the local administrator took all the factors into account, and his decision is based on a proper application of Chapter 842 and local regulations pursuant to that statute. Under this type of review, the appealing party can only add to the record if some facts were left out at the local administrative level or if the administrative decision was not based on law. Because it is a procedural review, the entire process can be completed in as little as 10 or 15 minutes, which is essential in Boston given the housing court's backlog and, of course, the desirability of swift determinations in rent-adjustment and eviction cases.

These factors lead the assistant administrator for evictions to suggest that, at least for Boston if not for all rent controlled communities, judicial review of local decisions should be limited by Chapter 842 to a Chapter 30-A type of on-the-record review.

Civil Remedies

No pertinent comments or observations were registered.

Criminal Penalties

The former administrator would like to see a provision added to Section 12 of Chapter 842 not unlike that part of Section 10 of Chapter 19 (Boston's ordinance controlling FHA rents) which makes it unlawful for any person to deprive a tenant of the peace, comfort, or enjoyment of his housing accommodations, to engage in any conduct resulting in a violation of the tenant's privacy, or to harass, intimidate, threat, or coerce the tenant.

Termination

Inflation is beginning to look like a long-term phenomenon in this country. The housing production problem does not appear to be solvable in the short term either. With these factors in mind, and the realization that statutes can always be repealed, there are strong grounds for making Chapter 842 permanent. At a minimum, the former Boston Rent Control Administrator believes it should be extended for five more years.

The rent control administration's general counsel feels that termination of Chapter 842 would result in the conversion of Boston into a "ghost town." The compliance officer similarly believes it would be a serious error to let Chapter 842 expire at the end of 1975. Statistics show that rent control in Boston has kept the city's rental inflation at half the national average at a time when Boston tenants' real incomes are declining. Continuation of rent regulation is essential, he believes.

Extension of Chapter 842 for a minimum of five years is essential if it is to be offered as a serious local option, points out the assistant administrator for rents, because no community will bear the startup costs in a program for which the state enabling statute has only a one- or two-year horizon.

3 Fair Net Return

Purpose

The method used to determine what constitutes a fair and reasonable rent is obviously of central importance to the rent-control process. A variety of computational methods are possible. In Massachusetts, as elsewhere, the selection and application of an appropriate computation methodology or formula has been left largely to the discretion of the individual localities which have opted for rent control. And, as might be expected, there are as many approaches to computing rent levels and adjustments as there are Massachusetts communities with rent control.

The purpose of this chapter is to examine these as well as other alternative approaches, identify various major strengths and weaknesses, raise key policy issues, and suggest possible areas for improvement.

Statutory Framework

Sections 6 and 7 of the Massachusetts Rent Control Enabling Act (Chapter 842, Acts of 1970) provide the principal—indeed only—statutory guidelines as to how localities are to compute rent levels for rent-control purposes. These two sections, taken together, stipulate that (1) a maximum rent shall be established for each controlled rent within a municipality at the time that the municipality first undertakes rent control; (2) that, with certain exceptions, the maximum rent shall be based on, and not exceed, the rent charged the tenant six months prior to the time that the municipality accepted rent control; (3) that the municipal rent control board or administrator may subsequently make individual or general adjustments in the maximum rent "as may be necessary to assure that rents for controlled rental units are established at levels which yield to landlords a fair net operating income for such units"; and (4) that the following factors, among others, should be considered by the board or administrator "in determining whether a controlled rental unit yields a fair net operating income."

1. Increases or decreases in property taxes.
2. Unavoidable increases or any decreases in operating and maintenance expenses.
3. Capital improvement of the housing unit as distinguished from ordinary repair, replacement, and maintenance.

4. Increases or decreases in living space, services, furniture, furnishings, or equipment.
5. Substantial deterioration of the housing units other than as a result of ordinary wear and tear.
6. Failure to perform ordinary repair, replacement, and maintenance.

Thus, while Chapter 842 defines the initial "maximum rent" with some specificity, it gives the local rent control board or administrator wide discretion in determining what adjustments should subsequently be made in such maximum rents. The only specific constraints on such discretion are that (1) the rent levels must allow landlords to earn a fair net operating income (FNOI) and (2) changes in maintenance and operating costs, service, and physical conditions must be considered in determining whether a given rent level will in fact yield the landlord a fair net operating income.

Basic Similarities in Computing Rent Levels

As might be expected, the latitude given to Massachusetts communities in determining how to establish appropriate rent levels and adjustments has led to a variety of different approaches. Yet all approaches have certain important underlying similarities. For example, all municipalities with rent control have adopted an essentially two-step process for calculating rent levels. Under this two-step process, the total rent for a given unit or set of units is broken down into two major components, and each component is dealt with separately. The first component consists of the various costs that are directly related to operating, maintaining, and managing the units in question and includes such items as superintendency, fuel, maintenance, renovation, other support, and property taxes. The other component is what Chapter 842 refers to as "fair net operating income." It includes so-called ownership expenses: interest, depreciation, contingencies, unallocated costs, income taxes, and profit. For discussion purposes, the first component will hereon be referred to as the allowable cost component and the second component as the FNOI component.

It should be stressed that not all of the costs listed above are divided among the two basic components in the same way by all municipalities. For example, as discussed further below, under the proposed Lynn formula, interest expense was treated as an operating expense rather than as an item of FNOI. Boston also allows interest on capital improvements as an operating expense. The important point, however, is that all municipalities do approach the computation of rent adjustments on an essentially two-step basis in which they attempt to deal with allowable costs and FNOI separately.

A second, and perhaps even more important, similarity among Massachusetts municipalities with rent control lies in the use of the "pass-through" concept for allowable costs. Under the pass-through concept, reasonable increases or decreases in allowable costs are added to, or subtracted from existing rents on a dollar for dollar basis. As indicated earlier, variations do exist both in the definition of what is an allowable cost and in the maximum amount that can be passed through at any one time. Some of the more significant differences (and similarities) as to what costs are and are not allowable are set forth in Table 3-1. Differences also exist in the use of ceilings and floors on cost pass-throughs. In Cambridge, on the one hand, no ceiling, per se, has been imposed on cost pass-throughs, provided of course that the costs are reasonable and allocable to the units in question. In contrast, both Boston and Somerville have imposed a ceiling of 10 percent on rent increases in any one year and in Somerville there is also a 12 percent floor on decreases.[a] In Brookline and Cambridge, landlords in the past have been encouraged to seek advisory opinions in advance of undertaking any significant capital improvements to learn what the allowable rents will be. Most municipalities give varying degrees of weight to the tenant's desires regarding the improvement in determining whether the improvement, and hence the amortized expense, is appropriate.

Computation of FNOI

As shown in Table 3-2, the five municipalities which have opted for rent control (Boston, Brookline, Cambridge, Lynn and Somerville) have at one time or another employed at least seven different formulas for computing FNOI. These seven formulas represent variations in four basic methods of calculating FNOI. For purposes of discussion, these four methods have been labeled the value method, the gross rents method, the fixed dollar method, and the equity method.

Value Method

Under the value method, FNOI is calculated as a predetermined percentage of property value. The value method is thus a form of return on gross assets. Two municipalities, Brookline and Somerville, currently use the value method, and a third municipality, Cambridge, did so in the past. As suggested in Table 3-2, the value formulas of the three cities, while conceptually similar, vary substantially both in the computation of property values and in the rate of return used. In Somerville, property value for FNOI computation purposes is based on the purchase price paid for the property in the last arms-length transaction and is adjusted for inflation incurred since the purchase date. In Brookline, on the

---
[a]Boston's ceiling was imposed only in individual cases.

Table 3-1
Allowable "Pass Through" Costs

Type of Cost	Boston	Brookline[a]	Cambridge	Somerville
Operating and maintenance (including utilities, fuel, insurance, and so forth).	Pass-through if incurred and reasonable up to 10% per year.	Pass-through if incurred and reasonable.	Pass-through if incurred and reasonable. No increase for non-recurring costs for code enforcement.	Pass-through if incurred and reasonable up to 10% per year increase or 12% decrease.
Management	6% maximum	6% maximum	Pass-through if incurred and reasonable.	Pass-through if incurred and reasonable.
Property taxes	Pass-through if incurred and reasonable.	Pass-through if incurred.	Pass-through if incurred and reasonable.	General increase given each year for tax increases.
Capital improvements subsequent to base date.	Pass-through of depreciation plus interest @ 8 1/2%.	Pass-through of straight-line depreciation, plus interest if a loan is taken out.	Pass-through of depreciation plus interest @ 9 1/2%.	Pass-through of straight-line depreciation for code enforcement and nonstructural improvements. No depreciation, but base value increased for structural improvements.
Depreciation for capital expenditures prior to base date.	Not allowed as cost pass-through. Considered part of FNOI.	Not allowed unless useful life still exists, in accordance with depreciation schedule.	Not allowed as cost pass-through. Considered part of FNOI.	Not allowed as cost pass-through. Considered part of FNOI.
Debt service: principal and interest.	Ditto	Ditto	Ditto	Ditto
Contingency allowance for cost increase, vacancies, bad debts, and so on.	Ditto	Ditto except for property taxes. (See above)	Ditto. Use of year end average rent for base year assumed to include contingency which carried forward in subsequent years.	Ditto
Profit	Ditto	Ditto	Ditto	Ditto

[a] Brookline does not allow cost pass-throughs in the same sense as Boston and Cambridge. In Brookline, incurred costs are deducted from gross income to arrive at net income which is then divided by value. Brookline audits the most recent 12 months' expenses.

Table 3-2
Methods for Determining Fair Net Operation Income

Method	NOI Formula	Computation of Base	Comments Regarding Base	Computation of Rate	Comments Regarding Rate
Value	Somerville: 4-10% of adjusted purchase price.	Purchase price adjusted for inflation, using Consumer Price Index for housing.	Incentive for owners to sell older homes unless maintain pre-roll-back price? Thus issue whether to adjust for inflation to present or only to roll-back date.	Rate of return earned in pre-control 1970 used. Rate held constant since purchase since 1970, use first mortgate interest rate.	20% reduction in rents for substantial and serious violations in building. 10% reduction for violations in building generally.
	Brookline: 6-11% of property value.	Formerly assessment values used. Resulted in fixed $ NOI as long as assessments remained same. Currently the following factors considered: –Purchase price if in last 3 years –Estimate of bona fide appraiser –LL testimony –5.5 gross income multiplier –1.45 x assessed value	Problem of rising property values caused by tight housing market. Brookline approach encourages resale to get higher valuation.	Formerly rate based on 3/70 rate (Regulations still so provide) Currently rate tied to quality of facility and services –6-7% for poor properties –8-9% for average properties –10-11% for good to excellent properties Rent increase almost automatic where property sold for higher price.	11% ceiling originally keyed to likely debt service limit. Regulations provide for periodic adjustment in ceiling rate but never done. Brookline board willing to agree in advance to rate increase in return for desired improvements.
	Old Cambridge #1: 10-15% of value. (Never adopted)	5x to 7x gross rents. Adjusted tax assessment and 3x assessed value used as check.	Regulations provided that 5x value be used for older buildings and 7x value for newer units.		Under regs, higher rate allowed for older buildings on theory that older building more risky. When combined with regs re: multiplier, result was to allow essentially the FNOI to all buildings with the same gross rents.
	Old Cambridge #2: 8-12% of value.	Same as above except that GOI as of 3/70 rather than current GOI used. Felt latter inflated by subsequent major rent increases.			

Table 3-2 (cont.)

Method	NOI Formula	Computation of Base	Comments Regarding Base	Computation of Rate	Comments Regarding Rate
	Possible: Net asset value.	Value computed as original cost x inflator less accumulated depreciation.	So-called RCNLD valuation method. Presumably depreciation would be allowed as an annual expense.		Should rate be based on pre-rollback date?
Gross Rents for cost plus	Old Boston: 40-50% of gross rents for elevator buildings, 30-40% for others.	Base for this formula is really allowable cost (NOI under old Boston formula = 67-100% of allowable costs for elevator buildings, 43-67% for others.)	Use of current gross rents will result in NOI rising faster than expenses. But NOI will not rise unless expenses do. A form of cost plus percentage of cost agreement. If converted to CPFF, becomes a "fixed dollar NOI."		
	New Cambridge: NOI earned in 1967 x Consumer Price Index for year-end.	Where reliable 1967 data unavailable, will use last subsequent year where data. Use 1.8 x allowable expense (based on 55:45 expense: NOI ratio) as a check. 1.8 factor applied to cost base.[a]	Overall Consumer Price Index used rather than index for Housing (see Somerville) in belief that LL uses earnings from units for own living expenses and these best reflected by general index.	None	Lack of use of % rate of return considered major advantage by some.
	New Boston: NOI as of 12/71.	20-50% of GOI used as test of reasonableness of 12/71 NOI. Also 30-35% taxes.	NOI for base year predicated on 100% occupancy. 35-50% GOI on buildings after 1959, 25-40% other buildings with 6 or more units; 20-35% other buildings with less than 6 units.		

Proposed Lynn: 8–12% of accumulated equity.	Equity = downpayment plus accrued mortgage principal.	Landlord receives more NOI as equity builds. Is this desirable? Pro: encourages long term ownership Con: tenants in effect pay for additional equity. May be difficult to determine LL equity. Formula requires constant recomputation. May discourage long term ownership by ignoring rising property values. LL may be able to increase equity by selling property at higher prices, purchasing new.	Some argue that ceiling needed both on NOI and on interest which is an allowable expense. Concerned over possible incentive to finance at higher rates. Might put ceiling on total of NOI plus interest, but allow relationship of two to vary.
	Possible alternative: Current value less outstanding mortgage.	Becomes a variation of value method. Tenants object to leveraging of inflated values.	
	Possible alternative: Base date value less base date mortgage plus subsequent principal payments.	Eliminates post-rollback date increases in value due to inflation but administratively difficult.	

[a] Only used where 1967 NOI cannot be established.

other hand, two quite different approaches have been taken in determining property value. During the first two years of rent control, the Brookline board relied principally on tax assessment values which had been reviewed and revised, in 1968, on the basis of 100 percent valuation. In recent months, however, the Brookline board has been moving away from its reliance on assessed values in the belief that such assessed values are becoming increasingly outdated. Instead, the Brookline board weighs recent prices paid for comparable properties and appraisal studies by outside appraisers. Emphasis is also given to the use of income multipliers (5.5 × gross income) and assessed value adjustment factors (1.45 × assessed value) in determining property values for FNOI computation purposes.

The value formulas formerly used by Cambridge closely paralled the Brookline approach. The Cambridge Rent Control Administration provided the following guidelines to determine the *market value* of a property:

1. Assessed valuation is generally between 25% and 40% of market value.
2. Between 5 and 7 times gross annual income equals market value.
3. As a rule of thumb, market value equals 3 times assessed value.

The administrative difficulties inherent in ascertaining fair market value certainly represent a potentially major drawback to the value method. Where, as was formerly true in Brookline, tax assessment values are reasonably uniform and up-to-date, or where, as in Somerville, landlords, tenants, and courts are willing to accept a simplified valuation scheme, the value method is certainly feasible. But where current valuation data are not available and/or where the various parties (most particularly landlords) are prepared to go to court over the value issue, the value method can become time consuming and expensive. In addition, there is some indication in recent court decisions that the courts may ultimately hold that the value method is basically incompatible with rent control. Indeed, in an earlier case (Wilson vs. Brown 137 F.2d 348) involving rent control during World War II, the Federal Circuit Court of Appeals agreed with the Federal Price Administrator that

"The use of market value as a test is inconsistent with the regulation of rents, because the value of the property on the market depends in large measure upon its earnings and inflated rents result in inflated market values. Nor do valuations by tax authorities furnish a satisfactory standard. Such valuations frequently reflect the application of inarticulate policies and assumptions which may be valid for tax purposes, but do not furnish a uniform basis for determining fair value."

In a more recent case, the Brookline Municipal Court, while not going so far as to reject all forms of the value method as a basis for rent control, did take the position that use of a valuation method based on a rent multiple (i.e., rental income × 5.5) resulted in a process of circular reasoning. The court stated in Henry Kaufman, et al. vs. Brookline Rent Control Board, et al. (Municipal Court of Brookline No. 893 of 1973) that

"Much of the evidence on the question of value was based upon formulas in which value was derived from fair economic rents. For reasons indicated in the Finding of April 26, 1974, this evidence was not considered to be of use in this inquiry which is to determine what is a fair rent level. The only basis for the Board's conclusion that the value was $52,000 was that $9,456, the present gross income under rent-control, multiplied by 5.5 yields $52,008. Again, for reasons indicated, a predetermined rent level cannot be the starting point of an inquiry to determine what rent level will yield an owner a fair net return on the value of his property. It must be concluded, therefore, that there was no substantial evidence before the Board to support its decision on the issue of market value."

The Third District Court of Eastern Middlesex, in Joan Ackerman et al. vs. William J. Corkery (Equity #17 of 1971), went even further:

"Nowhere in Chapter 842 is there a mention of 'Market Value.' There is no reference to market value of a property in determining the fair value of the landlord's investment. It is not mentioned in Section 7(b) as a factor to be considered. Yet the guidelines state that 'Investment should be taken as the current market value of the property.' By the guidelines the current market value of the property is considered as the most important element in the consideration of cases in which adjustments in the maximum rent are sought under Section 7 of Chapter 842.

"It seems clear from the wording of Chapter 842 and from the ruling of the Court in the Marshal House case that what is to be considered is a fair return on the landlord's property. If the fair return is to be based on market value, other elements than the landlord's investment are involved, such as the increased value which has arisen because of a substantial and increasing shortage of rental housing accommodations which result in the landlord receiving more than a fair return on his investment. It results in his getting the benefit of the emergency conditions which Section 1 of Chapter 842 gives as the reason for enactment of the act. The landlord's investment may well be and probably is much less than the market value. The result of the action of the Administrator has been to ensure to the landlords rents which exceed fair net operating income. The fair net operating income is not dependent upon market value, but would appear to be based upon operating expenses in relation to the [landlord's] investment which is not market value."

Like the value base, the other major variable in the value method equation, namely, the rate of return, is treated differently by different municipalities. As shown in Table 3-1, the allowable range of rate of return varies considerably. In Brookline, the range is 6 to 11 percent; in Somerville, 4 to 10 percent; and under the old Cambridge formula, 8 to 12 percent. Perhaps more significant are the differences in how the various municipalities select an appropriate rate within the allowable range for a specific unit or set of units. In Somerville, the board gives primary emphasis to the rate of return earned by the units in question during the latest prerent control period (1970) if the units were purchased prior to 1970. For units purchased after 1970, the board typically pegs the rate of return at the first mortgage interest rate for the units.

In Brookline, three quite different approaches have been tried. Initially the Brookline board followed the Somerville practice of allowing the same rate of return as was earned immediately prior to rent control.

Where insufficient data were available to verify the rate of return immediately prior to rent control, for example, where the property changed hands subsequent to rent control, the Brookline board used a sliding scale rate of return, ranging from 6 to 11 percent depending on the condition of the property. It might be argued that use of the debt service rate would have been inadequate if, as suggested earlier, FNOI includes not only principal and interest but also depreciation, contingencies, and net income or profit. The counterarguments are as follows. First, the principal repayment increment in the debt service charge in effect serves the same purpose as depreciation, namely, the recovery of capital investment, and that to the extent that the owner has invested his own capital in the property rather than borrowing, the principal increment accrues to him. An alternate approach used in New York City and in federal rent control programs is to treat depreciation as an allowable cost (New York allows a depreciation charge of up to 2 percent of the property value) and reduce the FNOI rate of return (New York allows 8 1/2 percent of assessed value or the latest bona fide purchase price). Similarly, it can be argued that the interest increment of the debt service charge also serves as a reasonable surrogate for profit. The reasoning here is that the amount of profit earned by the owner/investor should be directly related to the size of his investment and that this is most equitably achieved by including an increment in the FNOI equal to the annual interest on the total original cost, i.e., investment in the property. This total interest amount then accrues to the lenders as interest and to the owners as profit, depending on the proportion of debt and equity in the property. Finally, it can be argued that where the FNOI is based on the debt service rate applied to present market value, the use of present market value rather than original cost or investment as the base in effect provides the landlord with a cushion that can be used for contingencies or profit. To illustrate, assume purchase of a property on 1 January 1971 for $100,000 with a 75 percent mortgage coverage and an annual debt service of 9%. If the value of the property increases 10 percent/year over the next three years, the difference between the debt service rate applied to original cost and the debt service rate applied to current market value would be $2,979 (0.09 × $133,100 − 0.09 × $100,000). Carrying the example one step further, the total FNOI of $11,979 at the end of the third year would be divided as seen below.

Later, as the base values used for NOI computations began to rise, the board began to key the rate of return to assessed values in 1970. Finally, in the last few months, the board has begun implementing a policy which (1) keys rates to

Principal and interest payments to the lender (0.09 x $75,000)	$ 6,750
Amortization (or depreciation) of owner's investment (assume 25 year life)	1,000
Contingencies and profit	4,229
Total FNOI	$11,979

existing values and (2) adjusts the rates to reflect the physical quality and services of the units. In this latter regard, an informal sliding scale has been established which allows an 8 to 9 percent rate of return for an average building and higher or lower rates for better or worse than average buildings.

Fixed Dollar NOI Method

As the title suggests, the fixed dollar NOI approach bases the fair net operating income for a particular unit or set of units on the amount earned in a given period. Typically, this amount is equated to the amount earned in a base period prior to the establishment of rent control. For example, in Boston, the FNOI for units purchased prior to December 1971 is the same as the NOI earned in December 1971, provided that the actual NOI does not fall above or below certain prescribed percentages of gross operating income and taxes. Thus the FNOI for buildings built after 1959 must fall within a range of 35 to 50 percent of gross operating income.

The fixed dollar NOI approach currently used by Cambridge differs in three major respects from that of Boston. First, where appropriate cost data is available, the Cambridge Rent Control Administration uses the year 1967 rather than December 1971 as the base year for determining FNOI. Second, and more important, Cambridge adjusts the 1967 FNOI upward to compensate for the current lower purchasing power of the dollar. For this purpose, Cambridge uses the composite Consumer Price Index (as distinguished from the Consumer Price Index for Housing used by Somerville in adjusting purchase prices). Finally, for units for which reliable 1967 data are not available, Cambridge officials take the year for which such data are available and then apply the appropriate inflation factor for subsequent years. Boston, on the other hand, uses an alternate FNOI formula (percentage of gross rents), where appropriate data are not available for the base year due to a subsequent sale of the property.

Gross Rents Method

Under the gross rents method, FNOI is computed as a percentage of allowable costs, much as overhead is allocated under various types of accounting systems.

Only one municipality, Boston, has used the gross rents method although the old Cambridge approach came close to a gross rents formula. See Table 3-2. Under the former Boston approach (subsequently replaced with a fixed dollar NOI method), FNOI was calculated at 40 to 50 percent of gross rents (80 percent to 100 percent of expenses) for elevator buildings and 30 percent to 40 percent of gross rents (43 to 80 percent of expenses) for others. As indicated earlier, Boston still uses this formula for property purchased after December 1971.

The principal advantage of the gross rents method is administrative simplicity in that having once ascertained allowable costs, the rent control agency need only apply a predetermined factor to those costs to establish FNOI. The major drawback, on the other hand, is the disincentive for cost control since the higher the allowable cost base, the higher will be the FNOI.

Equity Method

Under the return on equity method, FNOI is computed as a percentage of the landlord's accumulated equity. Accumulated equity can, of course, be defined in various ways. In a strict accounting sense, equity is the difference between depreciated assets carried at cost and liabilities. Use of this definition for rent control purposes, however, obviously would pose serious administrative problems, since it would require construction of a balance sheet for each unit or series of units, a task undoubtedly unfamiliar to a large proportion of landlords. A simplified approach considered by Lynn would have defined a landlord's equity on a particular property as the total of his downpayment plus accrued mortgage principal.

Proponents argue that the equity method most accurately reflects the landlord's investment in a particular property and that hence it is intrinsically more fair to all concerned. On the other hand, the equity approach obviously imposes significantly greater administrative burdens on both the landlord and the rent control board or administrator both because of the additional data needed and because of the constantly changing nature of the landlord's equity. Moreover, it is certainly debatable whether the additional accuracy in computing the landlord's investment under the equity formula has any real advantage over other approaches which lump investor's profit and lender's interest together under FNOI and then let the investors and lenders decide how the amount should be divided up.

Comparative Analysis of the Various Methods

There are at least three major types of criteria against which the various rent computation formulas might be evaluated. The first is essentially one of equity between the landlord and the tenant, i.e., how and to what extent do the various formulas distribute the burden of inflation between landlord and tenants. The second criterion is one of effectiveness, i.e., how effective has the use of each formula been in achieving the ultimate purpose of rent control, namely, the control of rents. And finally, the third criterion involves administrative efficiency, i.e., what is the relative level of effort required to apply and administer each of the formulas.

Equity of the Formula for Landlord and Tenant

Perhaps the single most important difference among the various formulas currently in use rests in the underlying assumptions as to how the burden of inflation should be distributed between landlord and tenant. As noted earlier, under all methods and formulas currently in use, reasonable increases in allowable costs are passed through, dollar for dollar, to tenants in the form of higher rents. True, some cities have imposed a ceiling on pass-throughs that will be allowed in any one year, but this procedure simply defers any increase over and above the ceiling to a subsequent year. Thus, in all cities, the basic philosophy is that the tenant should bear the burden, in the form of higher rents, of any reasonable increases in allowable costs.

The various formulas for computing fair net operating income (FNOI), on the other hand, reflect fundamental philosophical differences regarding the impact of inflation. This is perhaps best illustrated through a comparison of the fixed dollar NOI approach as practiced by Boston, on the one hand, and the approaches of Brookline, Cambridge, and Somerville on the other. Under the Boston approach, the FNOI for any particular unit (barring any unusual circumstances) is based on, and equivalent to, the total dollars of NOI earned in December 1971. The Boston approach thus treats the landlord's return or income as essentially fixed, much like an investment in a bond. To the extent that the value of the dollar goes down, then the buying power of the fixed income derived by the landlord will also go down.

This decline in the real dollar value of the fixed income derived by the landlord may be somewhat aggravated by two factors. First, all cities with rent control permit individual adjustments only if the claimed increases in costs have already been incurred.[b] The only exception to this is in Brookline, where antici-

---

[b]The Cambridge Rent Control Administration maintains that by using average rents at the end of 1967 as its base, it has in effect allowed a contingency to be built into the base year NOI since the landlord presumably had adjusted his 1967 rents to reflect anticipated 1968 cost increases; and this contingency, once built in, gets passed along each year under the Cambridge formula. Two key assumptions obviously underpin this reasoning: first, that landlords did in fact include contingencies in their 1967 rent increases; and second, that the size of the contingency allowance so included would still be adequate in today's economy. The Cambridge Rent Control Administration also maintains that it would be prepared to allow additional FNOI if the landlord could show that the current FNOI was inadequate to cover contingencies. No such claims, however, have been raised to date.

pated tax increases may be allowed. Moreover, in no cases will rent adjustments for a future period include costs actually incurred but not covered by an offsetting rent increase in a prior period. Thus cost increases incurred prior to the granting of a rent adjustment must, in fact, be paid by the landlord from his net operating income. The second situation is somewhat analogous. As discussed earlier, some cities have imposed ceilings on the amount of costs that can be passed through to the tenant in any one year. Where such a ceiling is exceeded, the additional costs actually incurred over and above the ceiling will have to be absorbed by the FNOI.

Thus, under the Boston approach, the landlord quite clearly absorbs the impact of inflation on the FNOI increment of the total rent. As noted earlier, the tenant largely (but not totally) absorbs the inflationary impact of rising allowable costs. One can argue, of course, that while many tenants have received and continue to receive increases in wages and salaries which tend to offset rising rents caused by increased costs, landlords do not. On the other hand, many tenants who live in rent-controlled units, particularly the elderly, have essentially fixed incomes and for them, the burden of inflation is at least as great as for the landlords.

In contrast to the fixed dollar NOI approach of Boston, Brookline, Cambridge and Somerville (and the old Boston formula) have sought to adjust the FNOI to reflect changes in the value of the dollar. As discussed earlier, both Brookline and Somerville base FNOI on the value of the property in question. In the case of Brookline, value was initially based on the assessed valuation for tax purposes, but later was modified to include other valuation methods. Somerville, on the other hand, has computed property values, for rent control purposes, as a fraction of the original purchase price multiplied by an inflation factor keyed to the Consumer Price Index for Housing. Similar in result, though not in approach, were the old Boston gross-rents formula which in effect computed FNOI as a percentage of allowable costs and the Cambridge approach which adjusts the base year FNOI for subsequent inflation.

The issue of whether rent control is to be a temporary or long-term proposition is a basic policy question that the general court may well want to address in the statute. Alternatively, the long-term/short-term issue may be left to the localities to resolve, but statutory language included indicating which FNOI formula(s) may or may not be appropriate for the rent control time frame anticipated. A third alternative would be to say nothing in the statute about either the time frame or the FNOI formula issue, but provide for the development of state level implementing guidelines in these two issue areas.

Certainly, the general court should address the issue of the intended duration of rent control. We also see a need, at a minimum, for amplification of the statutory definition of FNOI so as to reduce the recent incursion of some courts into essentially administrative policy matters. For example, it would be useful for the general court to declare its intent regarding the practice of using various types of formulas for rent control purposes.

We also see a need for some form of state level guidelines which address in some detail both the computation of FNOI and the determination of the types and amounts of allowable cost pass-throughs. Such guidelines are needed to assure at least a minimum level of consistency, to avoid a "reinventing of the wheel" and repetition of the same mistakes by each municipality, and to provide a structure for building a body of consistent and supportive court decisions. We are inclined to feel that such state level guidelines might better take the form of administrative guidelines rather than statutory provisions because of the greater flexibility of the former.

Effectiveness of Various Formulas in Controlling Rents

A second major factor that obviously should be considered in evaluating various rent control formulas—and indeed in evaluating rent control as a totality—is the degree to which the various formulas in question have in fact been effective in holding rents down. Logically, the question of relative effectiveness should be readily determinable by a statistical trend analysis of average or median rents in various communities with and without rent control. Unfortunately, the only agency that we could find that has made a continuing effort over time to compile and maintain a comprehensive statistical data base of rent trends has been the U.S. Census Bureau and even there, the data base is updated only every ten years. Various of the Massachusetts communities with rent control have done little in the area of statistical trend analysis, although at least one, Brookline, has the requisite computer capability. We would strongly recommend in this regard that high priority be given to developing an appropriate statistical data base of rent trends in the commonwealth. This is presumably a function that the Massachusetts Department of Community Affairs might logically perform.

Administrative Efficiency

An important, albeit certainly not overriding, consideration in evaluating various FNOI formulas is the relative administrative ease or difficulty in applying each formula. Table 3-3 sets forth the cost per controlled unit incurred in 1973 in each municipality in administering rent control. Obviously, many factors other than the type of FNOI formula used have had an important bearing on the above unit costs. Brookline, for example, has a large investigative staff while Somerville has none. Similarly, Brookline (and Cambridge) holds a formal hearing on every petition while Somerville does not. And Brookline, for various reasons, receives a substantially higher percentage of individual adjustment petitions than does Somerville.

Table 3-3
Unit Cost of Local Rent Control Administration

Municipality	Number of Controlled Units	Total Administrative Costs	Cost/Unit
Boston	125,000[a]	$873,800	$ 6.99
Brookline	11,300[a]	$126,448	$11.19
Cambridge	20,424	$252,341	$12.36
Somerville	10,000[a]	$46,986	$ 4.70

[a]Estimates by local rent control boards.

While many of these factors influencing workloads and costs are thus largely unrelated to the particular FNOI formula being used, there is little doubt that the latter does have a substantial bearing on administrative costs. The executive director of the Brookline Rent Control Board, for example, cites a heavy load of court cases as a major contributor to Brookline administrative costs, and a principal issue of controversy in such cases has been the determination of property value. It is also apparent in reviewing the Brookline hearing records that the question of property value and the rate of return to be allowed on such value also consumes a substantial amount of hearing and staff support time.

In contrast, the Boston fixed dollar FNOI formula is relatively simple, unambiguous, and easily applied. The Somerville formula, though based on value, has also proved relatively simple to apply, largely because of the relative simplicity of the valuation formula.

Thus, some of the formulas have a clear advantage over others in terms of administrative ease of application. The differences, however, which produce these advantages are often ones of degree and would appear better dealt with, if at all, through administrative regulations rather than through statutory changes.

Appendix

Appendix A: Chapter 842 of the Acts of 1970

Chap. 842. An Act Enabling Certain Cities and Towns to Control Rents and Evictions.

Whereas, The deferred operation of this act would tend to defeat its purpose which is, in part, to alleviate the severe shortage of rental housing in certain areas of the commonwealth, which shortage has caused a serious emergency detrimental to the public peace, health, safety and convenience, therefore this act is hereby declared to be an emergency law, necessary for the immediate preservation of the public peace, health, safety and convenience.

Be it enacted, etc., as follows:

Section 1. *Declaration of Emergency.* The general court finds and declares that a serious public emergency exists with respect to the housing of a substantial number of the citizens in certain areas of the commonwealth but especially in the cities of the commonwealth regardless of population and towns with a population of fifty thousand or over, which emergency has been created by housing demolition, deterioration of a substantial portion of the existing housing stock, insufficient new housing construction, increased costs of construction and finance, inflation and the effects of the Vietnam war, and which has resulted in a substantial and increasing shortage of rental housing accommodations for families of low and moderate income and abnormally high rents; that unless residential rents and eviction of tenants are regulated and controlled, such emergency and the further inflationary pressures resulting therefrom will produce serious threats to the public health, safety and general welfare of the citizens of the aforementioned communities and in other communities adjacent to them; that such emergency should be met by the commonwealth immediately and with due regard for the rights and responsibilities of its local communities.

Section 2. This act shall take effect in any city and in any town with a population of fifty thousand or over, on the thirtieth day following acceptance of its provisions. A city or town which has accepted this act may, in like manner, revoke its acceptance.

Section 3. *Definitions.* The following words or phrases as used in this act shall have the following meanings:

(a) "Rental units", any building, structure, or part thereof, or land appurtenant thereto, or any other real or personal property rented or offered for rent for living or dwelling purposes, including houses, apartments, rooming or boardinghouse units, and other properties used for living or dwelling purposes, together with all services connected with the use or occupancy of such property.

(b) "Controlled rental units", all rental units except:

(1) rental units in hotels, motels, inns, tourist homes and rooming or boarding houses which are rented primarily to transient guests for a period of less than fourteen consecutive days;

(2) rental units the construction of which was completed on or after January one, nineteen hundred and sixty-nine, or which are housing units created by conversion from a nonhousing to a housing use on or after said date;

(3) rental units which a governmental unit, agency, or authority either:

(i) owns or operates; or

(ii) regulates the rents, other than units regulated (a) under the provisions of this act, or (b) under the provisions of chapter seven hundred and ninety-seven of the acts of nineteen hundred and sixty-nine and any act in amendment thereof or in addition thereto, or (c) under the provisions of any other general or special law authorizing municipal control of rental levels for all or certain rental units within a municipality; or

(iii) finances or subsidizes, if the imposition or rent control would result in the cancellation or withdrawal, by law, of such financing or subsidy;

(4) rental units in cooperatives;

(5) rental units in any hospital, convent, monastery, asylum, public institution or college or school dormitory operated exclusively for charitable or educational purposes; or nursing home or rest home or charitable home for the aged, not organized or operated for profit;

(6) the rental unit or units in an owner-occupied two-family or three-family house;

(7) that a municipality accepting the provisions of this act may exempt those rental units for which the rent charges exceeds limits specified by said municipality; provided that in no event shall more than twenty-five per cent of the total rental units in said municipality be exempted under this subsection.

(c) "Rent", the consideration, including any bonus, benefits, or gratuity demanded or received for or in connection with the use or occupancy of rental units or the transfer of a lease of such rental units.

(d) "Services", repairs, replacement, maintenance, painting, providing light, heat, hot and cold water, elevator service, window shades and screens, storage, kitchen, bath and laundry facilities and privileges, janitor services, refuse removal, furnishings, and any other benefit, privilege or facility connected with the use or occupancy of any rental unit. Services to a rental unit shall include a proportionate part of services provided to common facilities of the building in which the rental unit is contained.

Section 4. *State Assistance and Review.* (a) The department of community affairs shall establish a bureau of rental housing to assist municipalities which accept this act to carry out local rent control in a manner to best effectuate the provisions of the act and with due regard for the rights and responsibilities of the accepting municipality.

(b) The bureau of rental housing shall carry out studies and analyses, collect and publish data and information and render other assistance to municipalities which have accepted the provisions of this act or which propose to do so.

(c) Said bureau may advise a municipality which has accepted the provisions of this act that the local execution of rent control does not conform to the intent of this act.

Section 5. *Local Rent Board or Administration.* (a) At the time of acceptance of this act the city or town shall also determine in like manner whether the act will be administered by a rent control board or by a rent control administrator. Upon acceptance of this act and prior to its effective date, the mayor of a city, or the city manager in a city having a manager form of government, or the board of selectmen in a town shall appoint rent control administrator or a rent control board to serve at the pleasure of the appointing authority.

(b) Members of rent boards shall receive no compensation for their services, but shall be reimbursed by their city or town for necessary expenses incurred in the performance of their duties.

(c) Either the rent control board, hereinafter called the board, or the rent control administrator, hereinafter called the administrator, as the case may be, shall be responsible for carrying out the provisions of this act, and shall hire, with the approval of the appointing official or officials, such personnel as are needed, shall promulgate such policies, rules and regulations as will further the provisions of this act, and shall recommend to the city or town for adoption such ordinances and by-laws as may be necessary to carry out the purposes of this act.

(d) The board or the administrator may make such studies and investigations, conduct such hearings, and obtain such information as is deemed necessary in promulgating any regulation, rule or order under this act, or in administering and enforcing this act and regulations and orders promulgated hereunder. For the foregoing purposes, a person may be summoned to attend and testify and to produce books and papers in like manner as he may be summoned to attend as a witness before a court. Any person who rents or offers for rent or acts as broker or agent for the rental of any controlled rental unit may be required to furnish under oath any information required by the board or administrator, and to produce records and other documents and make reports. Such persons shall have the right to be represented by counsel, and a transcript shall be taken of all testimony and such person shall have the right to examine said transcript at reasonable times and places. Section ten of chapter two hundred and thirty-three of the General Laws shall apply, and for the purposes of this act a justice of the district court shall have the same power as a justice of the supreme judicial or superior court to implement the provisions of said section.

(e) The board or the administrator shall have the power to issue orders and promulgate regulations to effectuate the purposes of this act.

Section 6. *Maximum Rent.* (a) The maximum rent of a controlled rental unit shall be the rent charged the occupant for the month six months prior to the acceptance of this act by a municipality; provided that the rent board or the administrator of any municipality, wherein the rents are subject to regulation by any general or special law, may establish as a maximum rent the maximum rent, if any, established for rental units within such municipality by such general or special law. If the rental unit was unoccupied at that time but was occupied at any time prior to acceptance of this act, the maximum rent shall be the rent charged therefor for the month closest to six months prior to the effective date of the act. If the maximum rent is not otherwise established, it shall be established by the board or the administrator. Any maximum rent may be subsequently adjusted under the provisions of section seven.

(b) The board or the administrator shall require registration of all controlled rental units on forms authorized or to be provided by said board or administrator.

Section 7. *Maximum Rent Adjustment.* (a) The board or the administrator shall make such individual or general adjustments, either upward or downward, of the maximum rent established by section six for any controlled rental unit or any class of controlled rental units as may be necessary to assure that rents for controlled rental units are established at levels which yield to landlords a fair net operating income for such units. For the purposes of this section, the word "class" shall include all the controlled rental units within a municipality or any categories of such rental units based on size, age, construction, rent, geographic area or other common characteristics, providing the board or the administrator has by regulation defined any such categories.

(b) The following factors, among other relevant factors, which the board or the administrator by regulation may define, shall be considered in determining whether a controlled rental unit yields a fair net operating income:

(1) increases or decreases in property taxes;

(2) unavoidable increases or any decreases in operating and maintenance expenses;

(3) capital improvement of the housing unit as distinguished from ordinary repair, replacement and maintenance;

(4) increases or decreases in living space, services, furniture, furnishings or equipment;

(5) substantial deterioration of the housing units other than as a result of ordinary wear and tear; and

(6) failure to perform ordinary repair, replacement and maintenance.

(c) For the purpose of adjusting rents under the provisions of this section, the board or the administrator may promulgate a schedule of standard rental increases or decreases for improvement or deterioration in specific services and facilities.

(d) The board or the administrator may refuse to grant a rent increase under this section, if it determines that the affected rental unit does not comply with the state sanitary code and any applicable municipal codes, ordinances or by-laws, and if it determines that such lack of compliance is due to the failure of the landlord to provide normal and adequate repair and maintenance. The board or the administrator may refuse to grant a rent decrease under this section, if it determines that a tenant is more than sixty days in arrears in payment of rent unless such arrearage is due to a withholding of rent under the provisions of section eight A of chapter two hundred and thirty-nine of the General Laws.

(e) The board or the administrator may remove maximum rental levels, established under this section and section six, for any class of controlled rental units if in its judgment the need for continuing such maximum rental levels no longer exists because of sufficient construction of new rental units the rental levels for which are comparable to the rental levels of the class of controlled rental units for which maximum rental levels are to be discontinued or because the demand for rental units has been otherwise met. Any maximum rental level removed under this paragraph shall be reimposed or adjusted and reimposed upon a finding by the rent board or administrator that a substantial shortage of rental units exists in such city or town and that the reimposition of rent control is necessary in the public interest. Any action under this paragraph shall be subject to the hearing and notice requirements of paragraph (b) of section eight.

Section 8. *Rent Adjustment Hearings.* (a) The board or the administrator shall consider an adjustment of rent for an individual controlled rental unit upon receipt of a petition for adjustment filed by the landlord or tenant of such unit or upon its own initiative. The board or the administrator shall notify the landlord, if the petition was filed by the tenant, or the tenant, if the petition was filed by the landlord, of the receipt of such petition and of the right of either party to request a hearing. If a hearing is requested by either party, or if the action is undertaken on the initiative of the board or the administrator the hearing shall be conducted before the administrator or at least one member of the board prior to the decision by the board or the administrator to grant or refuse a rental adjustment. Notice of the time and place of the hearing shall be furnished to the landlord and tenant. The board or the administrator may consolidate petitions relating to controlled rental units in the same building, and all such petitions may be considered in a single hearing.

(b) On its own initiative, the board or the administrator may make a general adjustment, by percentage, of the rental levels for any class of controlled rental units within a municipality. Prior to making such adjustment, a public hearing shall be held before the administrator or before at least a majority of the board. Notice that an adjustment is under consideration, a description of the class of rental units which would be affected by the adjustment, and the time and place of said public hearing shall be published three times in at least one newspaper having a general circulation within the city or town.

(c) Notwithstanding any other provision of this section, the board or the administrator may, without holding a hearing, refuse to adjust a rent level for an individual rental unit if a hearing has been held with regard to the rental level of such unit within twelve months.

(d) Hearings required by paragraph (a) shall be conducted in accordance with the provisions of section eleven of chapter thirty A of the General Laws except that requirements (7) and (8) of said section eleven shall not apply to such hearings.

Section 9. *Evictions.* (a) No person shall bring any action to recover possession of a controlled rental unit unless:

(1) the tenant has failed to pay the rent to which the landlord is entitled;

(2) the tenant has violated an obligation or covenant of his tenancy other than the obligation to surrender possession upon proper notice and has failed to cure such violation after having received written notice thereof from the landlord;

(3) the tenant is committing or permitting to exist a nuisance in, or is causing substantial damage to, the controlled rental unit, or is creating a substantial interference with the comfort, safety, or enjoyment of the landlord or other occupants of the same or any adjacent accommodation;

(4) the tenant is convicted of using or permitting a controlled rental unit to be used for any illegal purpose;

(5) the tenant, who had a written lease or rental agreement which terminated on or after this act has taken effect in a city or town, has refused, after written request or demand by the landlord, to execute a written extension or renewal thereof for a further term of like duration and in such terms that are not inconsistent with or violative of any provisions of this act;

(6) the tenant has refused the landlord reasonable access to the unit for the purpose of making necessary repairs or improvements required by the laws of the United States, the commonwealth, or any political subdivision thereof, or for the purpose of inspection as permitted or required by the lease or by law, or for the purpose of showing the rental unit to any prospective purchaser or mortgagee;

(7) the person holding [occupancy] at the end of a lease term is a subtenant not approved by the landlord;

(8) the landlord seeks to recover possession in good faith for use and occupancy of himself, or his children, parents, brother, sister, father-in-law, mother-in-law, son-in-law or daughter-in-law;

(9) the landlord seeks to recover possession to demolish or otherwise remove the unit from housing use; and

(10) the landlord seeks to recover possession for any other just cause, provided that his purpose is not in conflict with the provisions and purposes of this act.

(b) A landlord seeking to recover possession of a controlled rental unit shall apply to the board or the administrator for a certificate of eviction. Upon receipt of such an application, the board or the administrator shall send a copy of the application to the tenant of the controlled rental unit together with a notification of all rights and procedures available under this section. If the board or the administrator finds that the facts attested to in the landlord's petition are valid and in compliance with paragraph (a), the certificate of eviction shall be issued.

(c) A landlord who seeks to recover possession of a controlled rental unit without obtaining such certificate of eviction shall be deemed to have violated this act, and the board or the administrator may initiate a criminal prosecution for such violation.

(d) Notwithstanding the provisions of this section the United States, the commonwealth, or any agency or political subdivision thereof, may maintain an action or proceeding to recover possession of any rental unit operated by it if such action or proceeding is authorized by the statute or regulation under which such units are administered.

(e) The provisions of this section shall be construed as additional restrictions on the right to recover possession of a controlled rental unit. No provision of this section shall entitle any person to recover possession of such a unit.

Section 10. *Judicial Review*. (a) Any person who is aggrieved by any action, regulation or order of the board or the administrator may file a complaint against the board or the administrator in a district court within the territorial jurisdiction of which is located the controlled rental unit affected by such action, regulation or order, and thereupon an order of notice shall be issued by such court and served on the board or the administrator. Such district court shall have exclusive original jurisdiction over such proceedings and shall be authorized to take such action with respect thereto as is provided in the case of the superior court under the provisions of chapter two hundred and thirty-one A of the General Laws, except that section three of said chapter two hundred and thirty-one A shall not apply. All orders, judgments and decrees of such district court may be appealed as is provided in the case of a civil action in such district court.

(b) The district court within the territorial jurisdiction of which is located the controlled rental unit affected shall have exclusive original jurisdiction over actions arising out of the provisions of section eleven.

Section 11. *Civil Remedies*. (a) Any person who demands, accepts, receives or retains any payment of rent in excess of the maximum lawful rent, in violation of the provisions of this act or any regulation or order hereunder promulgated, shall be liable as hereinafter provided to the person from whom such payment is demanded, accepted, received or retained, or to the municipality for reasonable attorney's fees and costs as determined by the court, plus liquidated damages in the amount of one hundred dollars, or not more than three times the amount by which the payment or payments demanded, accepted, received or retained exceed the maximum rent which could be lawfully demanded, accepted, received or retained, whichever is the greater; provided that if the defendant proves that the violation was neither willful nor the result of failure to take practicable precautions against the occurrence of the violation, the amount of such liquidated damages shall be the amount of the overcharge or overcharges.

(b) If the person from whom such payment is demanded, accepted, received or retained in violation of the provisions of this act or any rule or regulation hereunder promulgated fails to bring an action under this section within thirty days from the date of the occurrence of the violation, the board or the administrator may either settle the claim arising out of the violation or bring such action. Settlement by the board or the administrator shall thereafter bar any other person from bringing action for the violation or violations with regard to which a settlement has been reached. If the board or the administrator settles said claim, it shall be entitled to retain the costs it incurred in the settlement thereof, and the person against whom the violation was committed shall be entitled to the remainder. If the board or the administrator brings action under the provisions of this section, it shall be entitled to receive attorneys fees and costs under the provisions of paragraph (a) and the person against whom the violation was committed shall be awarded liquidated damages under said paragraph (a).

(c) A judgment for damages or on the merits in any action under this section shall be a bar to any recovery under this section in any other action against the same defendant on account of any violation with respect to the same person prior to the institution of the action in which such judgment was rendered. Action to recover liquidated damages under the provisions of this section shall not be brought later than one year after the date of the violation. A single action for damages under the provisions of this section may include all violations of the provisions of this section committed by the same defendant against the same person.

Section 12. *Criminal Penalties.* (a) It shall be unlawful for any person to demand, accept, receive or retain any rent for the use of occupancy of any controlled rental unit in excess of the maximum rent prescribed therefor under the provisions of this act or any order or regulation hereunder promulgated, or otherwise to do or omit to do any action in violation of the provisions of this act or any order or regulation hereunder promulgated.

(b) It shall be unlawful for any person to demand, accept, receive or retain any payment which exceeds the maximum lawful rent for one month as a finder's fee or service charge for the opportunity to examine or lease any controlled rental unit, and no finder's fee or service charge shall be lawful unless the person from whom the payment is demanded, accepted, received or retained actually rents or leases the controlled rental unit with regard to which payment of said fee or said charge has been demanded, accepted, received or retained.

(c) Whoever willfully violates any provision of this act or any rule or regulation hereunder promulgated, or whoever knowingly makes any false statement in any testimony before the rent board or administrator or whoever knowingly supplies the rent board or administrator with any false information shall be punished by a fine of not more than five hundred dollars or by imprisonment for not more than ninety days or both; provided, however, that in the case of a second or subsequent offense, such person shall be punished by a fine of not more than three thousand dollars or by imprisonment for not more than one year, or both.

Section 13. *Termination*. This act and all powers delegated herein shall terminate on April the first, nineteen hundred and seventy-five; provided that the provisions of this act shall be treated as still remaining in force for the purpose of sustaining any proper suit, action or prosecution with respect to any right, liability or offense arising under the provisions of this act.

Section 14. *Severability*. If any provisions of this act or the application of such provision to any person or circumstance shall be held invalid, the validity of the remainder of this act and the applicability of such provision to other persons or circumstances shall not be affected thereby.

Approved August 31, 1970.

Notes

Notes to Chapter 1
Statistical Evidence

1. Cambridge, Rent Control Report, March 1974.
2. *Public Housing Resources in Massachusetts*, Massachusetts Department of Community Affairs, March 1970.
3. Mr. George Hughes, Cambridge Housing Authority.
4. Mr. McCartney, Somerville Housing Authority.
5. The data in this section are based on figures from *General Housing Characteristics, Massachusetts*, U.S. Bureau of the Census, 1970, pp. 23-41.
6. "Net Spendable Earnings in Boston," published quarterly by the U.S. Department of Labor.
7. Eckert memo to the Revenue and Rent Control Committee.
8. Letter to Harbridge House, November 20, 1974.
9. The data in this section were obtained from "Why Rent Control Is Needed," Urban Planning Aid, Inc., Cambridge, Massachusetts, April 10, 1974 (pamphlet).
10. Ibid.

Bibliography

Achtenberg, Emily, *A Tenant's Guide to Rent Control in Massachusetts*, Urban Planning Aid, Inc., Cambridge, 1973.

———, *Less Rent, More Control*, Urban Planning Aid, Inc., Cambridge, 1973.

———, *Why Rent Control is Needed*, Urban Planning Aid, Inc., Cambridge, 1974.

Beissert, A.C., "New Jersey Considering Rent Control," *National Real Estate Investor*, Vol. 14, no. 4, April 1972, pp. 164-166.

Boston Redevelopment Authority, Planning Department, *A Preliminary Study of Boston Rent and Sales Prices*, 1960-1969, Boston, 1970.

DeSalvo, Joseph S., "Reforming Rent Control in N.Y.C.: Analysis of Housing Expenditures and Market Rentals." *Regional Science Association Papers*, Volume 27, Philadelphia, 1971, pp. 195-227.

Dreyfuss, David and Joan Hendrickson, *A Guide to Government Activities in New York City's Housing Markets*, Rand Corporation, Santa Monica, California, 1968.

Gaffney, Mason, "Land Rent, Taxation and Public Policy: Taxation and the Functions of Urban Land Rent," *The American Journal of Economics and Sociology*, vol. 32, January 1973, pp. 17-34.

Hayek, F.A. et al., "Verdict on Rent Control: Essays on the Economic Consequences of Political Action to Restrict Rents in Five Countries," Institute of Economic Affairs, London, 1972.

Keen, Howard, Jr. and Donald Raif, "Rent Controls: Panacea, Placebo or Problem Child," *Business Review*, Federal Reserve, Philadelphia, January 1974, pp. 3-11.

Kristoff, Frank S., *People, Housing and Rent Control in New York City*, City Rent and Rehabilitation Administration, New York, June 1964.

"Latest Decisions on Rent Controls." *U.S. News and World Report*, vol. LXXIII, no. 4, July 24, 1972, p. 66.

Lowry, Ira S., *Rental Housing in New York City*, Vol. I, Rand Institute, New York, 1970.

Moorehouse, J.C., "Optimal Housing Maintenance Under Rent Control," *Southern Economic Journal*, vol. 39, July 1972, pp. 93-106.

Olsen, Edgar O., "An Econometric Analysis of Rent Control," *Journal of Political Economy*, vol. 80, no. 6, November/December 1972, pp. 1081-1100.

Olsen, Edgar O., *The Effects of a Simple Rent Control Scheme in a Competitive Housing Market*, Rand Corporation, Santa Monica, 1969.

Rasch, Joseph, *Landlord and Tenant, New York City Rent Control with All Amendments through January 1, 1972*, Lawyers Co-Operative Publishing Company, Rochester, 1972.

Rental Statistics, Based on Returned Rent Control Registration Statements,

Report prepared by Staff Assistants of the Brookline Rent Control Board, April 29, 1971.

Rosenthal, Howard, "Rent Control Laws," *Journal of Property Management*, vol. 39, no. 6, November-December 1974, pp. 273-274.

Stein, Andrew et al., *Report on Housing and Rents of the Temporary State Commission on Living Costs and the Economy of the State of New York to the Governor and the Legislature*, New York, January 1974.

Sternlieb, George, *The Urban Housing Dilemma: The Dynamics of New York City's Rent Controlled Housing*, New York City Housing and Development Administration, New York, 1972.

About the Author

Herbert L. Selesnick, project director for this study, is a principal of Harbridge House, Inc. He received the bachelor's degree in physics, the master's degree in management, and the doctor of philosophy degree in political science from the Massachusetts Institute of Technology. A member of the National Association of Housing and Redevelopment Officials, he is the co-author of a January 1974 *Journal of Housing* article, "How Can You Tell What a Relocation Program Is Accomplishing?" In his capacity as Community Development Coordinator of Peabody, Massachusetts, he advises the mayor of that city on all phases of housing, transportation, and urban redevelopment policy.